Alfred's
Teach Yourself To Pedal Steel Guitar

JOE STOEBENAU

Everything you need to know to start playing now!

Alfred, the leader in educational publishing, and the National Guitar Workshop, one of America's finest guitar schools, have joined forces to bring you the best, most progressive educational tools possible. We hope you will enjoy this book and encourage you to look for other fine products from Alfred and the National Guitar Workshop.

This book was acquired, edited and produced by Workshop Arts, Inc., the publishing arm of the National Guitar Workshop.
Nathaniel Gunod, managing and acquisitions editor
Ante Gelo, music typesetter
Timothy Phelps, interior design
CD recorded by Colin Tilton at Bar None Studios, Northford, CT.
Interior photographs by Timothy Phelps.

Cover photographs courtesy of Carter Steel Guitars.

ISBN 0-7390-3595-9 (Book & CD)

CONTENTS

🎵 **Track I**

A compact disc is included with this book. This disc can make learning easier and more enjoyable. The symbol at the top appears next to every example that is on the CD. Use the CD to help ensure that you're capturing the feel of the examples, interpreting the rhythms correctly, and so on. The track number next to the symbol corresponds directly to the example(s) you want to hear. Track 1 will help you tune your pedal steel guitar to the CD.

ABOUT THE AUTHOR

Joe Stoebenau holds a bachelor's degree in music production and engineering from Berklee College of Music in Boston, Massachusetts, and is also a graduate of the Musician's Institute in Hollywood, California, where he studied guitar.

Playing music for more than 25 years, Joe is proficient on several instruments. In addition to pedal steel guitar, he plays Dobro, French horn, harmonica, guitar, lap-steel guitar, trumpet and flugelhorn. Currently residing in Pennsylvania with his wife and three basset hounds, Joe is also the author of *Teach Yourself to Play Dobro* and *Christmas for Harmonica* available from the National Guitar Workshop and Alfred Publishing Co., Inc.

PHOTO BY: TIMOTHY PHELPS

The author would like to thank the following people for making this book possible: Nat Gunod, Tim Phelps and the staff at Workshop Arts, L.C Harnsberger, Alfred Publishing, Ken Gehret, Marty Bonk, Bruce Heffner and Collin Tilton at Bar None Studios.

INTRODUCTION

The pedal steel guitar can turn a sad song into a real tear-jerker, take a Texas roadhouse song and make it jump and swing and, when the signature "crying" sound is used, it can make just about any song sound "country."

The purpose of this book is to give you the foundation, basic skills and knowledge needed to play the pedal steel guitar. This foundation is simply that—a place from which to begin building. Upon completion, you will have the basic skills to play with a band and to learn your favorite songs. It is from these experiences that you will continue to learn and develop as a musician.

The pedal steel guitar is a fascinating instrument; its possibilities are endless. Whichever style of music you prefer—country, rock, jazz, blues or even classical music—there is a place for the pedal steel guitar. It is also a continuously evolving instrument. It has developed very quickly in less than 50 years and we can only guess where it will be in the future.

As you begin this book, move ahead slowly and be sure to assimilate the material before moving on to the next section. Each chapter is a building block for the next. You may have heard that the pedal steel is a difficult instrument to learn, but this is only true when it is approached without direction. In writing this book, my goal was to provide the direction you need to approach learning the pedal steel logically while having some fun along the way.

So, get out your pedal steel, crack open your favorite beverage and begin to *Teach Yourself to Play Pedal Steel Guitar*.

GETTING STARTED A BRIEF HISTORY OF THE PEDAL STEEL GUITAR

The pedal steel guitar as we know it today has a long history dating back to Hawaii in the late 1800s. It was from there that some of the first accounts of musicians sliding a piece of metal, such as a knife blade, across the strings of their instruments come.

As this technique evolved, the Dopyra brothers invented the *resonator guitar* in 1920. This instrument, which they called the Dobro, looks like a traditional acoustic guitar, with a body constructed of either wood or metal, but has an aluminum resonator. A resonator, which looks a lot like a speaker from a modern-day radio or stereo, amplifies the sound of the guitar. Hawaiian musicians embraced the instrument, and due to its square neck and high action, played it flat on their laps using a metal bar called a *steel*. There have been many manufacturers of resonator guitars but two of the most popular have been Dobro and National. Both of these companies have undergone many changes of ownership but continue to produce resonator instruments.

The advent of amplifiers and electric guitars in the 1930s was another very important step in the development of the steel guitar. Initially, magnetic pickups were added to existing guitars. This worked fairly well but it was found that a body made of solid wood worked better because it reduced the problem of feedback. This led to the development of the solid body steel guitar. This instrument became known as the *lap steel* guitar because guitarists rested it on their laps while sitting down. Also, the *table steel* guitar came along. This had anywhere from one to four necks, was supported by legs and played from a standing position. The purpose of the multiple necks was to allow for different tunings, making the guitar more versatile.

By the end of World War II, double-neck, eight-string steel guitars became popular and in the 1950s, players started adding pedals to pull certain strings to higher pitches.

Webb Pierce's song, "Slowly," was a turning point for the steel guitar. It featured a steel player named Bud Isaacs and was the first recording to include the use of pedals.

Throughout its early development, the tuning of the steel guitar was anything but standard. Each player had his or her own favorite tunings that worked for the style of music they were playing. The late 1950s found Shot Jackson, Jimmy Day, Ralph Mooney and many others working to develop a configuration for the pedal steel guitar that would become standard.

In 1964, a young steel player named Buddy Emmons developed tunings that would become, for the most part, "standard." The pedal steel guitar became an instrument with one or two ten-string necks with one neck tuned to *E9 chromatic* (this became known as *Nashville tuning*) using three pedals, and the other neck tuned to *C6* and using five or more pedals. The neck tuned to C6 is known as the *jazz neck* and is used a lot on western swing music.

This standardization helped manufacturers of steel guitars to increase their sales, and one of the largest companies was Sho-Bud founded by Shot Jackson and Buddy Emmons. Their instruments had become the aesthetic and tonal standard. Since this time, many great pedal steel guitar companies have continued to develop the instrument. These include MSA, The Emmons Guitar Company, Sierra Guitars, Carter Guitars and many others.

GETTING STARTED PARTS OF THE PEDAL STEEL GUITAR

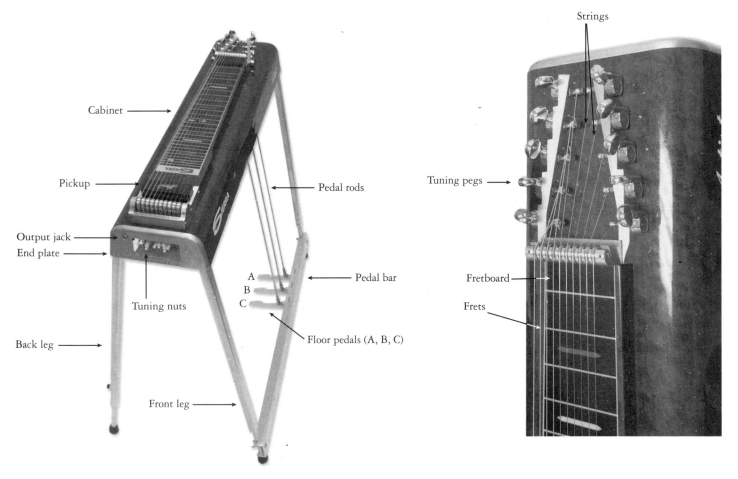

Cabinet

Pickup

Output jack

End plate

Tuning nuts

Back leg

Front leg

Pedal rods

Pedal bar

A
B
C

Floor pedals (A, B, C)

Strings

Tuning pegs

Fretboard

Frets

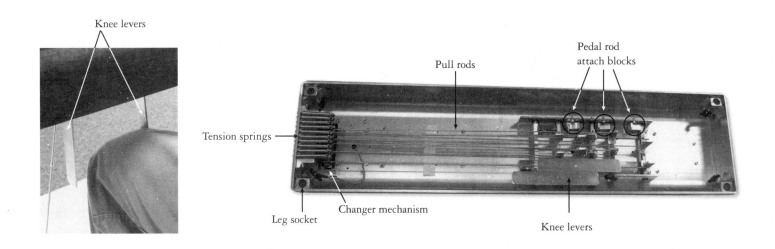

Knee levers

Tension springs

Leg socket

Changer mechanism

Pull rods

Pedal rod attach blocks

Knee levers

GETTING STARTED THE COMPLETE PEDAL STEEL SETUP

Amplifiers

In addition to the pedal steel guitar, an amplifier is needed to produce the sound of the guitar at a level that can be heard. When starting out, a large amplifier is not needed. There are a number of small practice "amps" made for the electric guitar on the market that will work quite well. As you progress in your abilities and begin playing with other people in a band, a larger amplifier will be needed. Because the pedal steel has a wide range, both harmonically and dynamically, try to find an amplifier that has at least 80 to 100 watts of power and a 12- or 15-inch speaker. A *solid state* amp will work better than a *tube* amplifier. Solid state amps are made up of transistors in circuits which reproduce the sound of the steel very well. Tube amps, while preferred by some electric guitar players, use vacuum tubes which color the sound and don't reproduce the bright sound of the steel guitar as well.

Volume Pedal

A *volume pedal*, controlled by the right foot, is commonly used to control a pedal steel guitar's volume to the amplifier. There will be more about volume pedal technique later in this book (page 62). There are volume pedals made specifically for both steel guitars and electric guitars. Pedals made for the steel guitar generally sound better as they are designed with the instrument's wide range in mind. A volume pedal is not needed to start playing the steel guitar so if economics dictate, add it to your setup later.

Seat

Just about any kind of armless seat will work when starting to play the steel guitar. Make sure it is low enough for you to get your knees under the guitar. Generally, light-weight piano and drum seats work very well. There are seats made specially for the pedal steel guitar which include storage for volume pedals, cables and other items.

GETTING STARTED ASSEMBLING YOUR PEDAL STEEL

The exact instructions for assembling a pedal steel guitar may vary from model to model and from manufacturer to manufacturer. Check the instructions that came with your instrument before proceeding.

1. With the case open and facing you, remove the *pedal bar* and bag containing the *legs*. Leaving the guitar body in the case, lay out the legs and pedal rods.

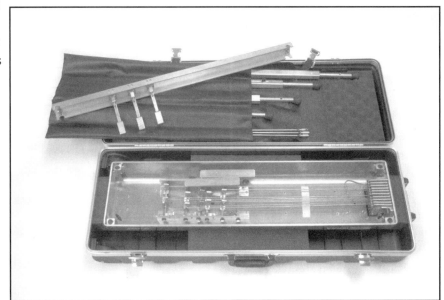

2. Identify the two legs that will support the pedal bar (if available, check the instructions that came with your guitar). Inspect the legs near the feet. In most cases, there will be *mounting holes* for the *pedal bar bolt* to go through. Insert these legs into the front (logo side) leg holes in the guitar body, making sure the bolt holes near the feet are oriented to receive the pedal bar.

3. Next, install the pedal bar on the front side of the legs by sliding the bolts through the holes in the legs and tightening the wing nuts, being careful not to make them too tight.

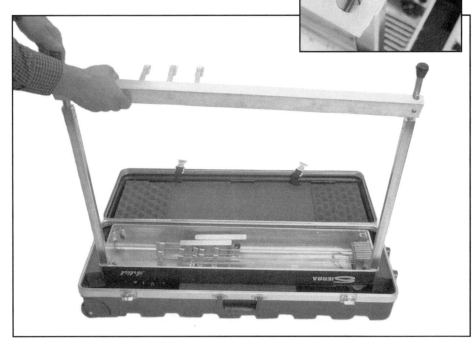

4. Lay out the *pedal rods* and notice they are labeled "1," "2" and "3." Starting with rod "1," hook curved end into the hole on the *actuator assembly* nearest the tuning head. Install the other end over the *ball joint* on the corresponding pedal. Follow this by installing the other two pedal rods in order.

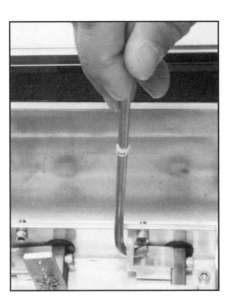 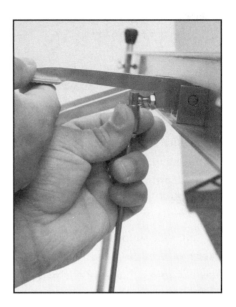

5. Install the two *back legs* next and pull the *knee levers* up into position.

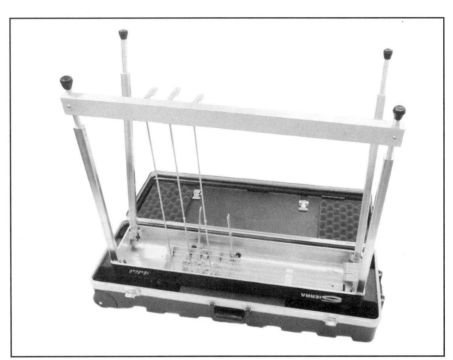

6. Lift the guitar up out of the case by grabbing hold of the legs at opposite corners and rotating it to an upright position as you lift. Use caution as some steel guitars can be quite heavy.

 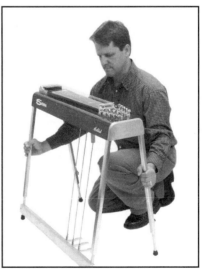

GETTING STARTED PLAYING POSITION

The pedal steel guitar is played from a sitting position. You will need to find a seat (see page 7). You should be able to slide both knees under your guitar with both feet resting flat on the floor. Your legs will be moving up and down a little, so leave room!

Your left foot should be placed just in front of the "B" pedal (center) so that you can reach any of the pedals without much movement. The right foot will be resting squarely on top of the volume pedal.

Sit far enough away so that your arms are bent comfortably at the elbows, but not so far that you are reaching for the guitar. Also, it is important not to sit too close and slouch over the guitar, as this can limit hand movement and cause back pain.

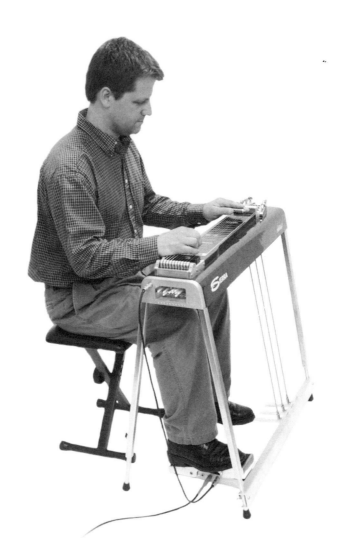

GETTING STARTED   PICKS

Pedal steel guitars are generally played fingerstyle with two metal *fingerpicks* and a plastic *thumbpick*. The fingerpicks are worn on the index (*i*) and middle (*m*) fingers of the right hand. They should fit snug and be stiff. Thicker picks (.025 inch) seem to work best. Rounded tips are preferable. The thumbpick should fit snugly on the thumb.

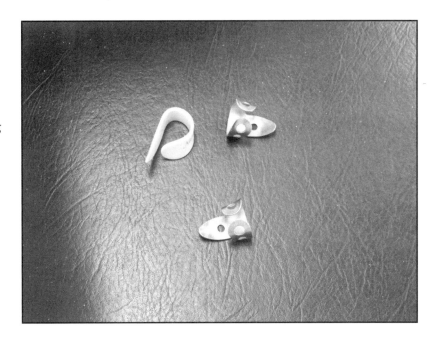

The Steel

The metal rod used to play the pedal steel guitar is called a *steel* or *bar*. There are many types to choose from, but for pedal steel you should use a *bullet nose* steel of medium weight made for a ten-string guitar. The steel is held in the left hand with the index finger pointing down the center, the thumb on the right side and the middle finger angled down the left side. The remaining fingers rest on the strings behind the steel for dampening purposes.

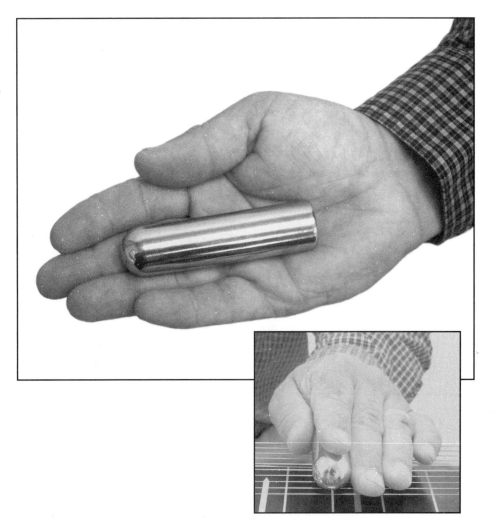

THE HANDS

The Fingers

The left-hand fingers are used to hold the steel and dampen the strings behind it. The individual fingers are not used to play the notes, as on a traditional guitar.

The right-hand fingers are used to pluck the strings, and are often indicated with the letters *T*, *i* and *m*, as in the fingerstyle tradition.

T = thumb
i = index
m = middle

Left-Hand Position

The left hand should be holding the steel across the strings parallel to the *fret lines*. Be careful to avoid using too much pressure. In most cases, the weight of the steel and the hand is enough pressure to keep from getting any buzzing sounds or other unwanted noises. To sound the correct pitch and be in tune, you must position the steel directly over the desired fret line.

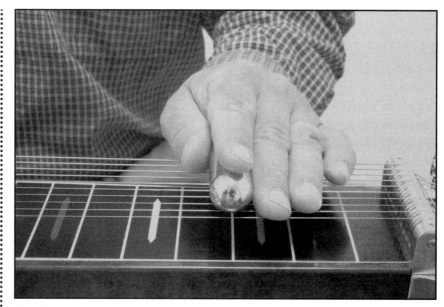

The left-hand fingers.

Right-Hand Position

The right hand is the picking hand and should be positioned near the bridge with the palm and 5th finger (pinky) side of the hand laying across the strings parallel to the fret markers.

The ring and 5th finger can be curled slightly to mute the treble strings (as shown in the photo).

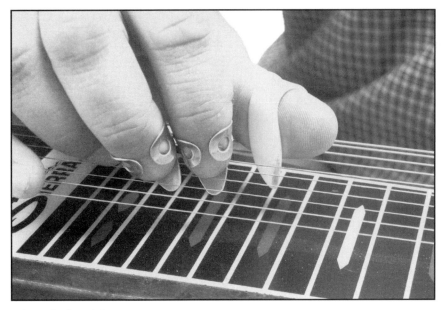

The right-hand fingers.

TUNING THE STRINGS

Whether playing music by yourself or in a group with others, having your instrument in tune is a very important first step.

The Musical Alphabet

To begin tuning your pedal steel guitar, you must know that every *pitch* (the degree of highness or lowness of a musical sound) has a letter name from the *musical alphabet*. The musical alphabet has seven letters that repeat:

A–B–C–D–E–F–G, A–B–C–D–E–F–G, A–B... and so on.

The notes in the musical alphabet represent the *natural notes*, which means that they have not been altered in any way.

We can alter a note by playing it one fret higher, or one fret lower. A distance of one fret is called a *half step*.

A note played one fret higher than its natural position is called a *sharp*.

This is a sharp sign: ♯

A note played one fret lower than its natural position is called a *flat*.

This is a flat sign: ♭

These signs are called *accidentals*.

Look at the neck of your guitar. If you place your steel over the 3rd fret of the 1st (highest) string and pluck, you will sound the note A. If you move your steel one fret higher to the 4th fret, you will sound an A♯ (A-sharp). If you move your steel one fret lower to the 2nd fret, you will sound an A♭ (A-flat).

E9 Chromatic Tuning

The most common pedal steel tuning is E9 chromatic tuning. It developed out of the work of the early steel players. They had used a variety of tunings, sometimes two or more together, on two-, three- and even four-neck steel guitars.

From the 10th, lowest string up, the notes are:

```
10 9  8  7  6  5  4  3  2  1
B  D  E  F♯ G♯ B  E  G♯ D♯ F♯
```

Let's take a look at the different ways available to tune your pedal steel guitar.

1. Use the accompanying CD for the tuning notes. **Track 1**

2. A pitch pipe, keyboard or another in-tune pedal steel guitar may be used to supply the correct pitches.

3. An electronic tuner is the recommended choice for tuning your pedal steel guitar. It is the most accurate and easiest way to tune. These devices come in all shapes and sizes and are available at most music stores. NOTE: Be sure to obtain a *chromatic tuner*, which will be able to tune all the notes on your pedal steel guitar.

Using an Electric Tuner

1. Begin by connecting the electronic tuner to your guitar's output jack with a standard phono jack cable.

2. Pick the 10th (lowest) string (B) and adjust the corresponding tuning key so that the needle on the tuner is centered with a B indication. Always listen to the string as you tighten or loosen the string with the tuning key. This will help avoid string breakage as a result of over-tightening.

3. Pick the 9th string (D) and use the tuner in the same manner.

4. Continue across the strings until all ten strings have been tuned.

Tuning to a Keyboard

The following diagram shows where the notes of the open string pitches lay on the piano. You may use a piano and this chart to tune your pedal steel guitar if you do not have an electronic tuner.

Notice that unlike the traditional guitar, the 1st string is not the highest string. The 3rd string is actually higher than the 1st and 2nd strings, and the 4th string is higher than the 2nd string.

String numbers: 10   9 8   7 6   5   2 4   1 3

(piano diagram)

B   D E   F♯ G♯   B middle C D♯   F♯ G♯   E

GETTING STARTED TUNING THE PEDALS

The electronic tuner will also be used in tuning the pedals. Find the special tuning tool that came with your guitar. This tool is placed over the individual pedal rod ends that are exposed on the right side of your guitar.

NOTE: The positions of the rods are not standardized and may vary from one pedal steel guitar to the next.

1. With the A pedal depressed, pick the 10th string (B). Adjust the corresponding pedal tuning rod so that the note is a C♯ (with the pedal still depressed).

> A quick way to figure out which pedal rod to adjust is to move the pedal up and down a few times and notice which rod or rods are moving in and out. While doing this, select the moving rod that matches the string/pedal combination you are trying to tune.

2. Continue to press down the A pedal and pick the 5th string (B) and adjust the corresponding pedal tuning rod as above.

3. Depress the B pedal and pick the 6th string (G♯). Tune the pedal as above by adjusting the pedal rod so that it matches the note A on the tuner.

4. Pick the 3rd string (G♯) with the B pedal depressed and tune to the note A as above.

5. Press down the C pedal and pick the 5th string and tune to the note C♯ by adjusting the pedal rod.

6. With the C pedal depressed, pick the 4th string and tune it to the note F♯.

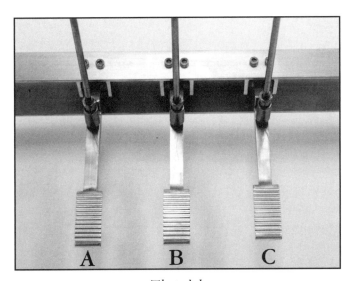

The pedals

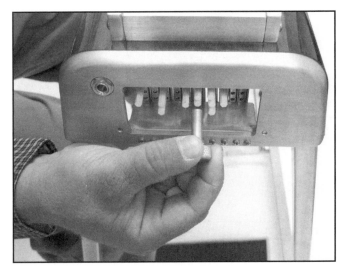

Using the special tuning tool to tune the pedals.

GETTING STARTED TUNING THE KNEE LEVERS

1. Push the E knee lever (right side, left knee) and pick the 8th string. Tune it to the note E♭ by adjusting the corresponding tuning rod.

2. With the E knee lever still pushed, pick the 4th string and tune it to the note E♭ as above.

3. Push the F knee lever (left side, left knee) and match the 8th and 4th strings to the note F on the tuner by adjusting the tuning rod. Notice that the knee levers move the pitch of the 4th and 8th strings both up and down.

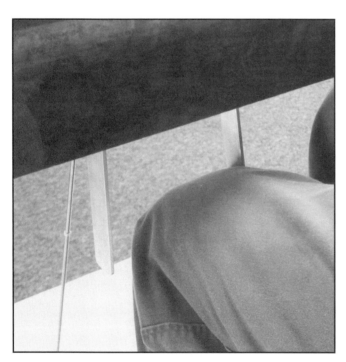

Pushing the E knee lever.

Pushing the F knee lever.

GETTING STARTED — THE PEDAL STEEL FRETBOARD

Below is a diagram of the fretboard. It can be used as a handy reference for the notes on the pedal steel guitar.

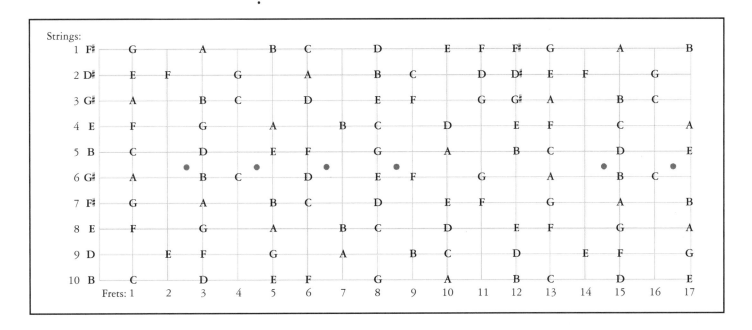

GETTING STARTED — PEDAL STEEL TABLATURE

Tablature, commonly known as TAB, is a notation system that shows us on which strings and frets to place the steel. It is read from left to right and has 10 lines representing the strings. The 1st string is represented by the top line. The lowest 10th string is represented by the bottom line. Numbers are placed on these lines to represent the fret to be played. As can be seen below, letters are sometimes placed beside fret numbers. These are pedal markings. Depress the indicated pedal when playing the fret. For example, the last note below is the 5th fret of the 3rd string with the B pedal depressed.

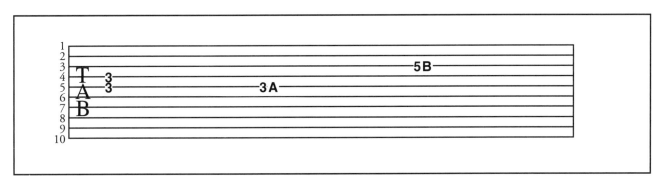

Bar Lines and Measures in TAB

Bar lines are vertical lines in the TAB. They divide the music into divisions of musical time called *measures*, which are groups of *beats*. Musicians often refer to measures as "bars," because bar lines create the measures. A beat is the basic unit of musical time. A *double bar* denotes the end of a section or short example. A heavier *final double bar* is used at the end of a piece or song.

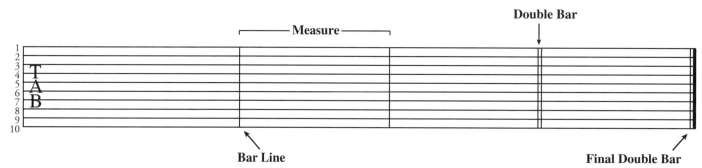

Playing Your First Notes

Your first notes will be picked with *T* (the thumb). To pick with *T*, push your thumb away from your body and drag the tip of the thumbpick across the desired string. Count aloud and tap your foot to keep time. There are four beats in each measure, so count "1, 2, 3, 4." When you are able to do this slowly, gradually speed up to a moderate *tempo* (speed).

HELPFUL HINT   When picking, it will be easier and sound better if you attack the string with the tip of the pick, as opposed to "digging in" and placing the pick too far down below the string.

Picking with *T*

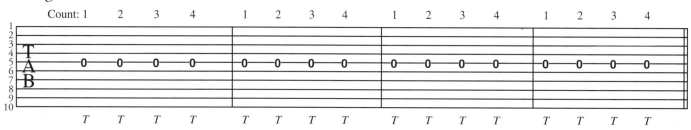

Next, practice picking with your (index) finger. Draw your finger across the string towards your body.

Picking with *i*

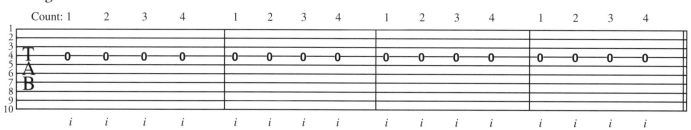

Repeat Signs

Repeat signs are used to indicate when a song, or portion of a song, should be played again. A *left-facing* repeat sign means to follow these steps:

1. Go back to the beginning and play again, or go back to the last right-facing repeat and play again.

2. Continue past the left-facing repeat to the end, or the next left-facing repeat.

Right-facing repeat   Left-facing repeat

We will start off playing our first song, "Two String Blues," by picking with both *T* and *i*. Play through it slowly at first and be sure to count evenly.

Two String Blues Track 2

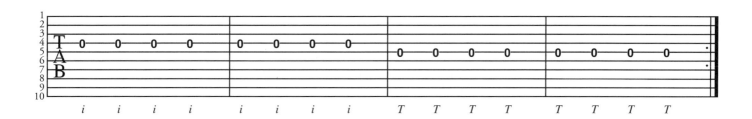

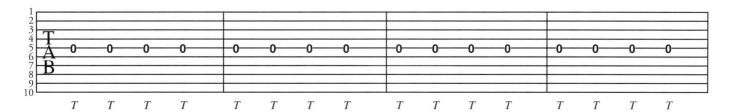

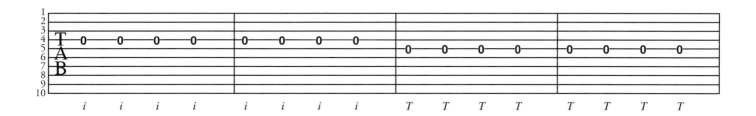

If every note in a song had the same duration, it wouldn't be very interesting. On this page, we will play some notes that take up the whole bar, four beats, as in bars 1, 2, 5, 6 and 8 below. Simply pick the note once and let it ring for four beats as shown.

We will also play some notes that take up one half of a bar, two beats, as in bars 3, 4 and 7. Pick the note and let it ring for two beats.

Counting Exercise   Track 3

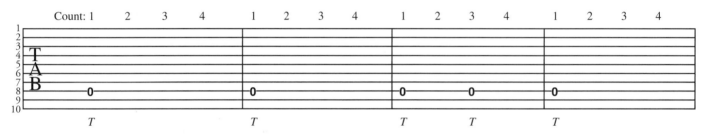

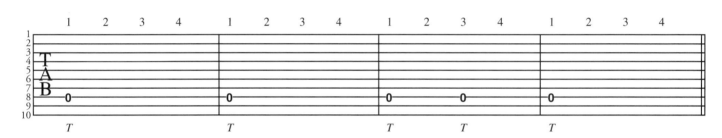

Using the Pedals

This next exercise is a brief lesson on using the A and B pedals.

We will begin with the pedal on the left side, which is the A pedal, and the center pedal, which is the B pedal.

When a new note is played by depressing the pedal instead of picking the string again, it is connected to the previous note in the written music with a *slur*, which is a curved line.

To use the pedals, pick a note on the string that pedal operates and, using your left foot, push down on the pedal to raise the pitch. This is a big part of what characterizes "the pedal steel sound." Have fun!

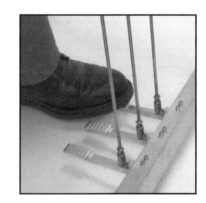

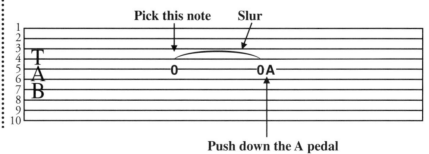

Pick this note   **Slur**

Push down the A pedal

HELPFUL HINT   Remember, the pedal to use will be notated in the TAB after the fret number.

> **HELPFUL HINT** When you change from one string to another, use the palm of the right hand—which is positioned by the bridge—to dampen the strings. This will keep one string from ringing through another.

Pedal Song Track 4

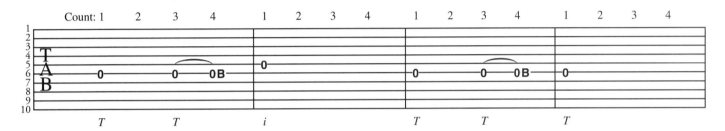

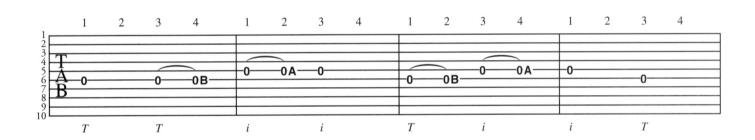

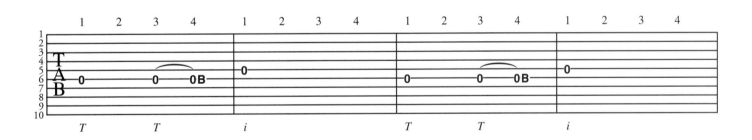

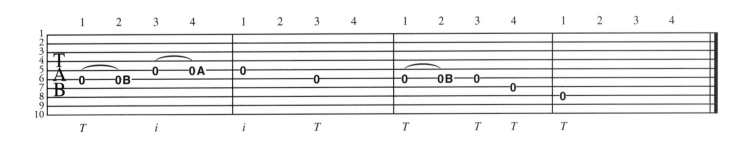

GETTING STARTED · READING STANDARD MUSIC NOTATION

Although not absolutely necessary for playing the pedal steel guitar, having a working knowledge of standard music notation is an important step toward being a well-rounded musician. Being able to read and interpret the musical language will enable you to communicate with other musicians as well as play a piece of music from the written page for your own enjoyment.

Music is written on a *staff*, which is made up of five lines and four spaces that are named with letters from the musical alphabet. At the beginning of the staff is a *treble clef*. It is also called the *G clef* because, by encircling the second line, it tells us that line is called G, thus telling us the names of all the lines and spaces.

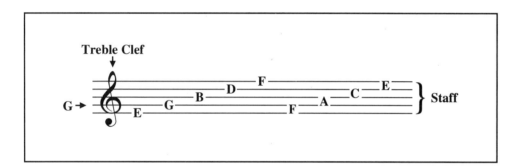

Lines and Spaces
Here are easy ways to remember the names of the lines and spaces:

Lines—From the lowest line to the highest, the notes on the lines are E, F, G, B, D and F. Use this phrase to remember those letters:

Every Good Boy Does Fine

Spaces—From the lowest space to the highest, the notes in the spaces spell the word

FACE

Notes

Music is written by placing *notes* on the lines and spaces of the staff. Notes appear a number of different ways.

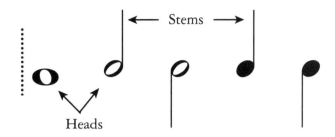

The notes on the staff are read alphabetically as they move up and down the staff from line to space as shown below. They are named according to the name of the line or space on which they appear.

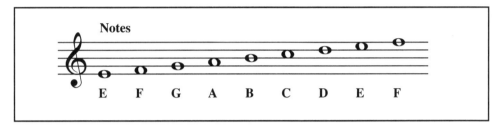

DeWitt "Scotty" Scott

Known as the "ambassador of the steel guitar," Scotty (as he is known to everyone) has single-handedly done more to promote the steel guitar than anyone else. Through his store, Scotty's Music, he has made just about every guitar, book, recording, and accessory related to the pedal steel guitar available to people around the world.

Scotty is the founder of the International Steel Guitar Convention held every year in St. Louis, MO. This is the largest steel guitar show in the world, attracting more than 3000 visitors and over 100 performers from many different countries.

Always looking for additional ways to promote the steel guitar, he formed his own record label, Mid-Land Records, which features artists of the steel guitar.

Scotty has authored several instructional books, numerous pedal and lap steel solos, and has also recorded his own albums. In addition, he has received numerous awards for his tireless efforts to help advance the steel guitar and is an honorary member of just about every steel guitar club and association around the globe. Scotty was inducted into the Steel Guitar Hall of Fame in 1992.

Beats, Note and Rest Values

As you know by now, duration, or musical time, is measured in beats. Beats are evenly pulsing units of time, like a heartbeat. And like a heartbeat, they keep the music alive. There are several types of notes with varying durations, which can be distinguished from one another by their appearance. Each note value has a correlating rest value. Rests are used to indicate silence. As we will see on the next page, each of these note and rest values has its own duration in beats.

The whole note or rest is the longest commonly used note value.

A half note or rest is half the value of a whole note or rest.

A quarter note or rest is half the value of a half note or rest. It is one quarter the length of a whole note; hence the name.

The diagram below shows how these three note and rest values relate.

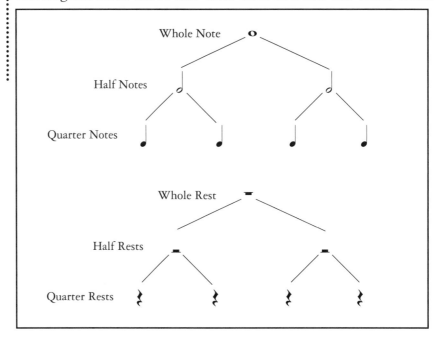

Bar Lines and Measures
As in TAB, bar lines are used on the staff to divide the staff into measures, a double bar line denotes the end of a section or short example and a heavier final double bar is used at the end of a piece or song.

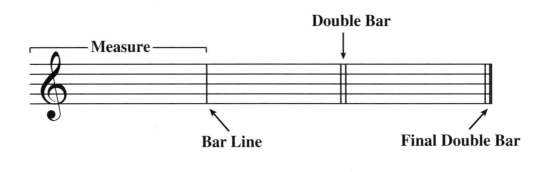

Time Signatures

At the beginning of every piece of music there are two numbers stacked on top of each other. These numbers are called the *time signature*. The top number tells us how many beats are in each measure. The bottom number tells us which note value receives one beat.

4/4   4 beats per measure
Quarter note ♩ = one beat

3/4   3 beats per measure
Quarter note ♩ = one beat

If a quarter note gets one beat, then a half note gets two and a whole note gets four. Let's update the note value diagram from page 24 with this new information.

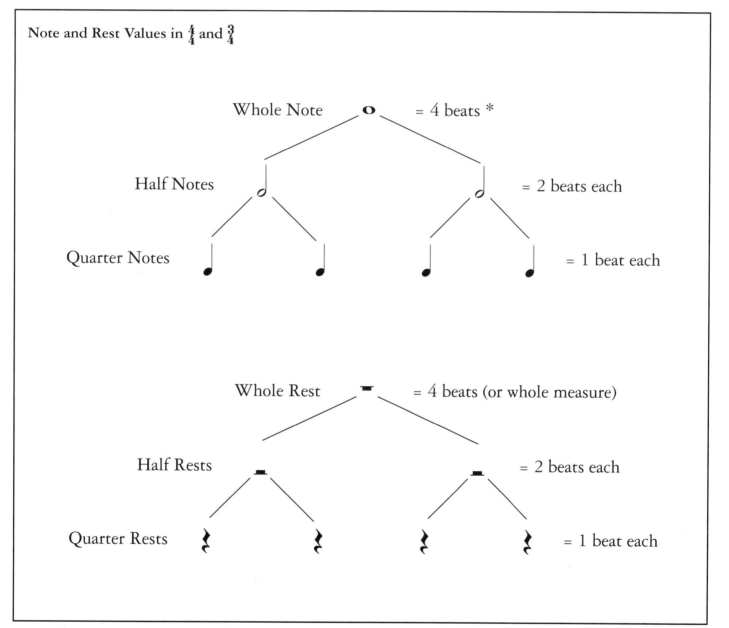

Note and Rest Values in 4/4 and 3/4

Whole Note — = 4 beats *

Half Notes — = 2 beats each

Quarter Notes — = 1 beat each

Whole Rest — = 4 beats (or whole measure)

Half Rests — = 2 beats each

Quarter Rests — = 1 beat each

* Whole notes do not occur in 3/4.

GETTING STARTED **RHYTHMS** Track 5

A *rhythm* is a pattern of note (and rest) values. It is often the rhythm of a song that catches and pleases our ears.

Below are some examples of basic rhythms. Count aloud and clap them until they are comfortable. Tap your foot as you count. This will help you feel the beats.

Rhythm Exercise No. 1

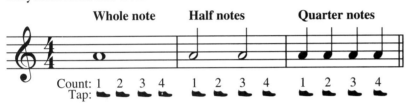

Rhythm Exercise No. 2

Rhythm Exercise No. 3

Rhythm Exercise No. 4

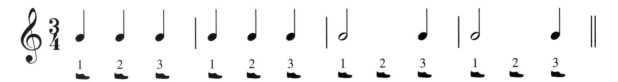

Rhythm Exercise No. 5

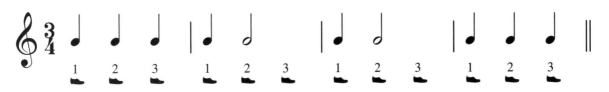

PLAYING SINGLE NOTES

The following lessons will take the most commonly used strings and consider them one at a time so you can learn to read and play the notes within the first five frets.

MINI MUSIC LESSON

Accidentals

Notice that in standard music notation, accidentals are placed just before (to the left of) the notes to which they apply. Also, remember this very important rule: an accidental is only in affect for the measure in which it appears.

Notes on the 3rd String G♯

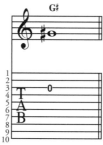

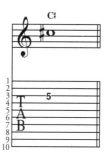

Play this 3rd-string exercise. Most of the notes are half notes.

Exercise on the 3rd String Track 6

Notes on the 4th String E

Here is an exercise for the 4th string. Play slowly at first. Notice that this exercise is mostly quarter notes.

Exercise on the 4th String   Track 7

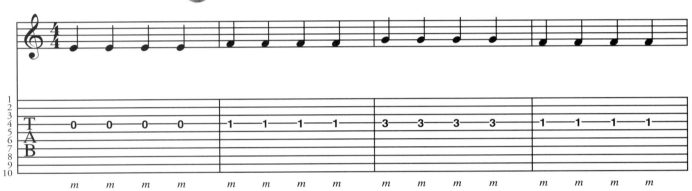

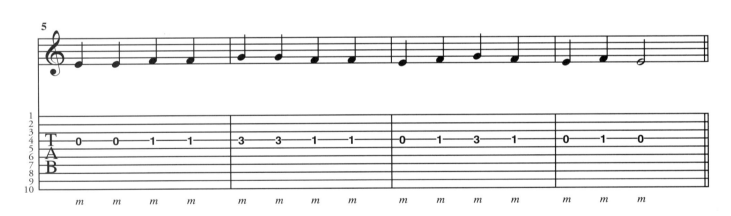

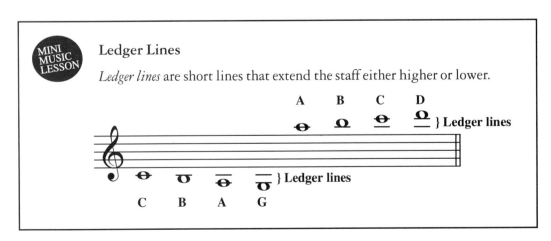

Ledger Lines

Ledger lines are short lines that extend the staff either higher or lower.

Notes on the 5th String B

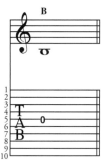

Notice that a ledger line is used for both B and C.

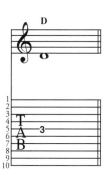

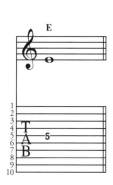

This 5th string exercise mixes half notes and quarter notes. Count carefully!

Exercise on the 5th String Track 8

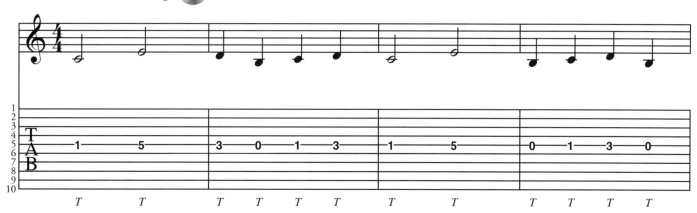

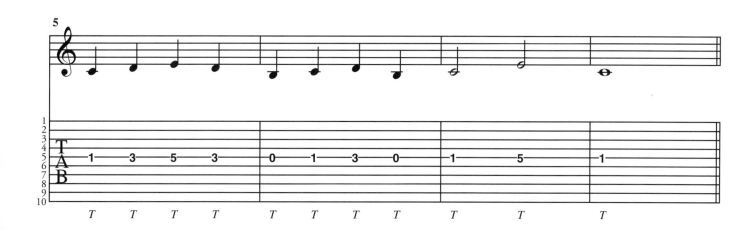

This song uses the notes learned on the 3rd, 4th and 5th strings. Take your time, learn it slowly and be sure the steel is centered directly over the fret so the notes will be in tune.

Ties
The duration of a note can be extended by attaching it to another note of the same pitch with a curved line ⌣ . This is called a *tie*. This is handy when the desired duration will not fit in the measure. In the TAB, a tied note is written in parentheses. When playing tied notes, attack the first note and let the sound carry over to the connected note; in other words: don't pick the tied note. See the last two measures of "Playin' Three Strings" for an example of a tie.

Playin' Three Strings Track 9

High C on the 3rd String

C Major Scale

Congratulations! You now know enough notes to play the *C Major scale*. This is a big accomplishment, because the major scale is a very important musical idea. The major scale will be covered in depth later in this book (page 42). For now, here's something fun to play using these notes.

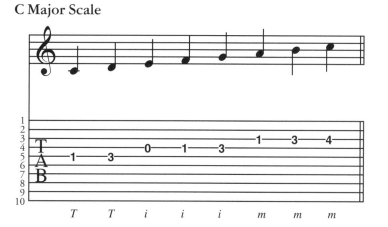

Scaling Mount C   Track 10

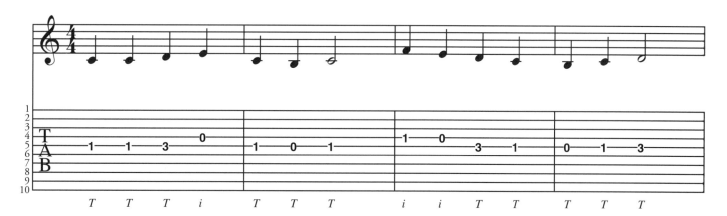

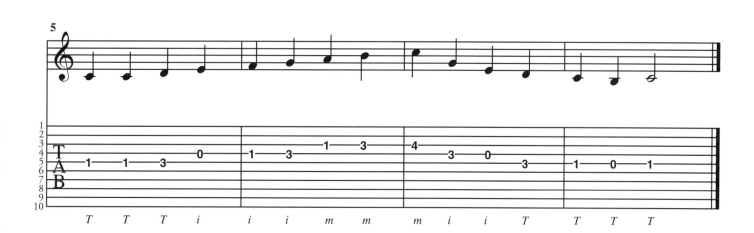

Notes on the 6th String G#

Exercise on the 6th String **Track 11**

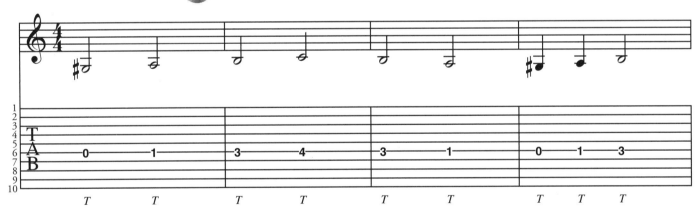

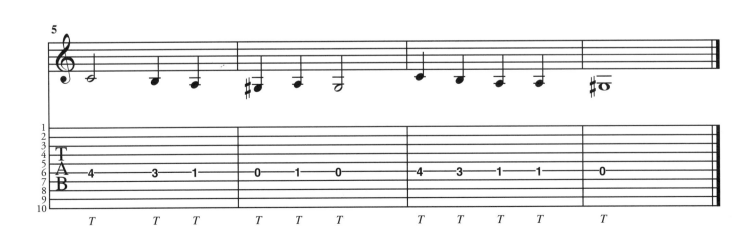

This classic melody uses lots of the notes we have learned. Take your time and learn it slowly, making sure to mute the strings with the right hand at the string changes.

The letters written above the music are *chord symbols*. These are provided so that a friend or your teacher can accompany you. Have fun!

Roll In My Sweet Baby's Arms   Track 12

Low G on the 8th String

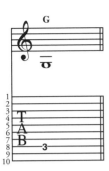

Here's a classic bluegrass tune for you
to play using your new note, low G.

Boil Them Cabbage Down 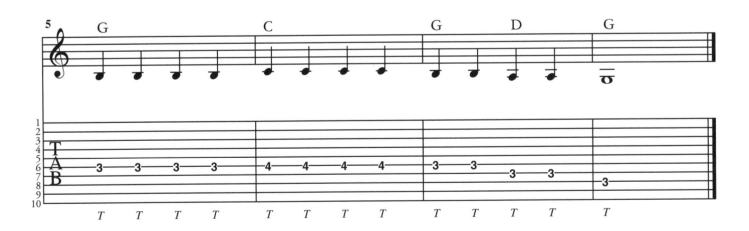 Track 13

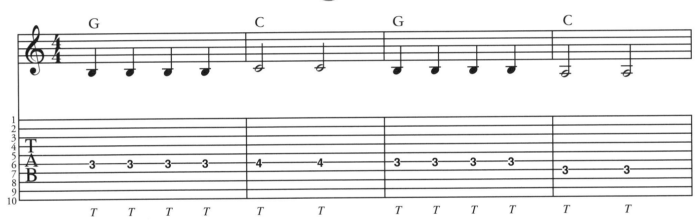

DOUBLE STOPS

One of the characteristic sounds of the pedal steel guitar is achieved by playing two notes together. These are called *double stops*.

The following exercises will help you coordinate your right-hand fingers to play simultaneously. Be sure to have the steel centered over the fret to keep the notes in tune.

Double-Stop Exercise   Track 14

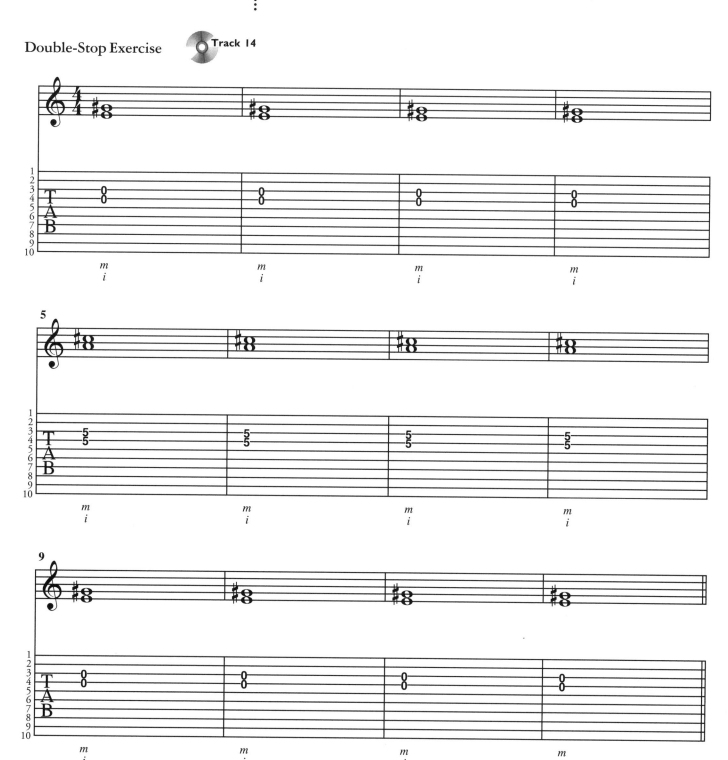

SLIDES

A *slide* is a *legato* sliding sound. Legato means "smoothly connected." A slide is performed by sliding the steel up or down the string(s) to create a gliding sound. When sliding, the note that you slide into does not have to be picked unless an attack is desired. A *slur* ⌣ is used to show that the second note in a slide is not picked.

Diagonal lines in the standard music notation and TAB, and an "SL" above the TAB, will tell you when to slide.

Slide up   Slide down
SL   SL

This example uses a slide on the 10th string. Be careful not to allow too much of the steel to hang off the guitar.

Slide Exercise 1 **Track 15**

You can also slide more than one note at a time. This is an excerpt taken from "Double Slippery" on page 37.

Slide Exercise 2 **Track 16**

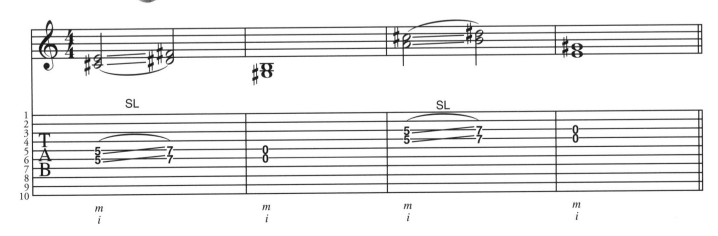

This song uses double stops and slides. Be careful to mute unwanted strings to keep it sounding clean.

Double Slippery  Track 17

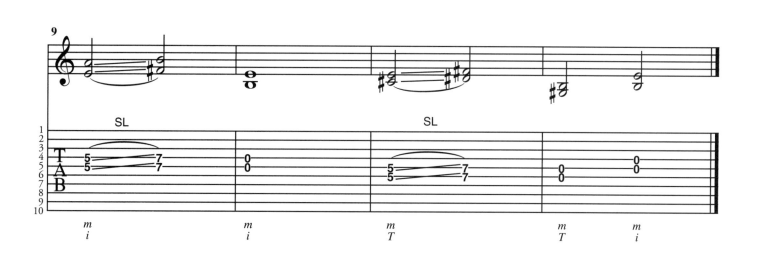

STRING GROUPS

Think of the 3rd, 4th and 5th strings as a *string group* and the 4th, 5th and 6th strings as another string group. These groups of strings are where you will play most of your melodies and harmonies.

A string group generally includes three strings. In the case of this book, the strings groups will be as follows:

3–4–5
4–5–6
5–6–8
6–8–10

8vb = *Ottava bassa*. Sounds an *octave* (12 half steps/frets) lower than written.

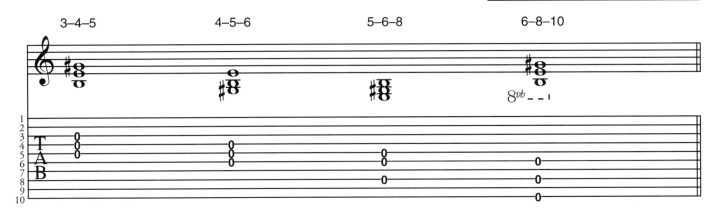

When playing a group of three notes, *T* plays the lowest note, *i* plays the middle note and *m* plays the top note. Pluck the strings simultaneously. When you want the sound to stop, simply rest the side of your right hand on the strings to keep them from vibrating. Another word for this technique for playing string groups is *blocking*. Play through these examples very slowly to get a feel for how your fingers need to move. As you progress through this book, you will find yourself using these "grips" time and time again, so learning them slowly now will help insulate you from picking up any bad habits later.

Blocking Exercise 1   **Track 18**

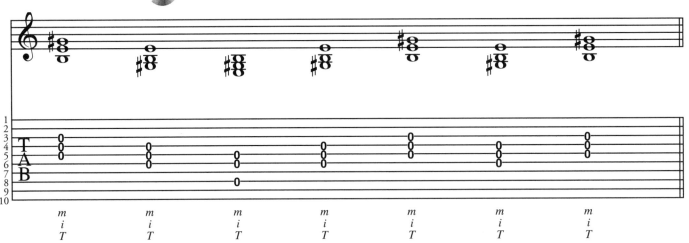

If you have trouble getting your fingers to the correct strings, don't worry. Slow down and take it one string, one finger at a time. You have to train your fingers where to go.

Taking your time and going slowly will help you progress more quickly. Picking will eventually become easier as you progress through this book.

Blocking Exercise 2  Track 19

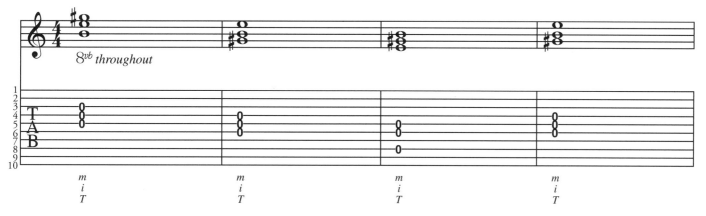

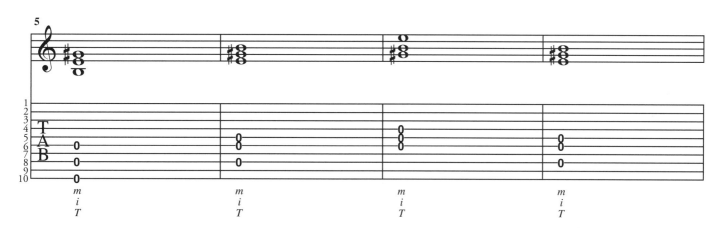

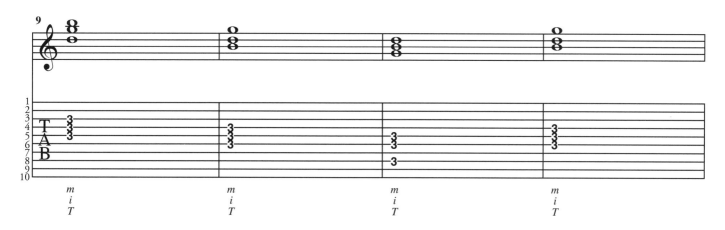

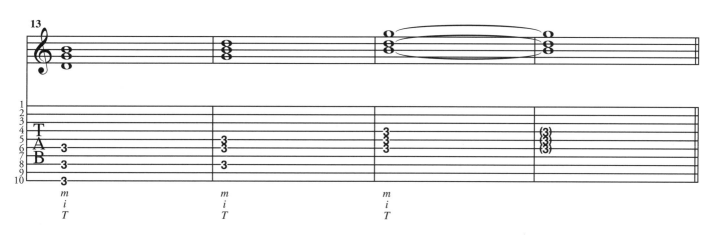

New Note on the 4th String: A   **New Note on the 6th String: C#**

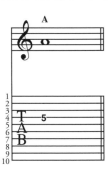 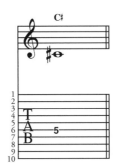

The following song will use the 3–4–5 and 4–5–6 string groups. Notice that we move up to the 5th fret in bar 9 and play the same groups. Proceed slowly to get the feel of moving from one string group to the next without letting unwanted strings ring.

Steel Groups Track 20

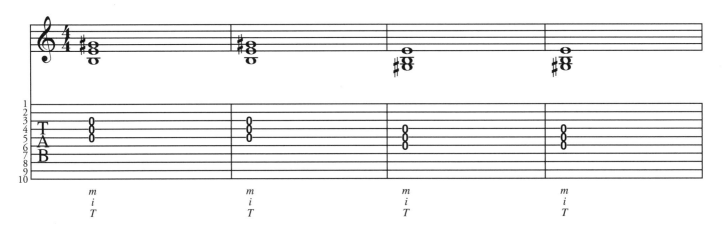

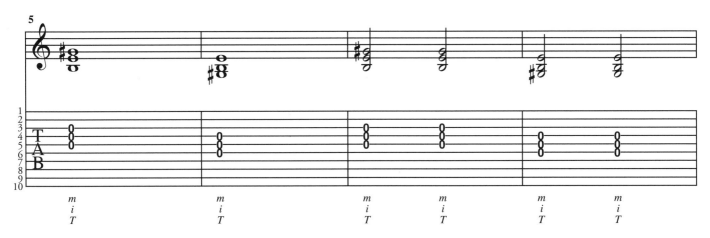

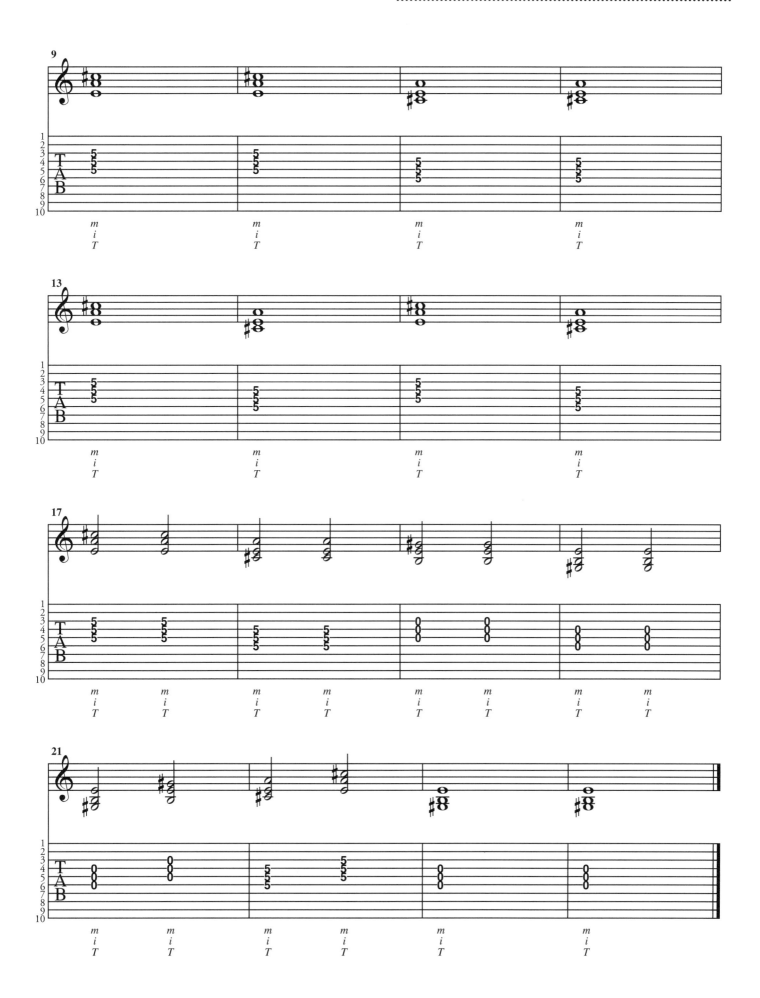

THE MAJOR SCALE

A *scale* is a series of notes in alphabetical order. It is a musical tool used to make melodies. Knowing how scales are constructed and learning some basic scale positions is an important part of being a well-rounded musician and playing the pedal steel guitar.

The *major scale* is the most widely-used scale. It is heard in every style of music from classical to jazz to country to reggae, rock and bluegrass. The major scale has been used to create the melodies of countless songs.

Half Steps and Whole Steps
To understand scales, you must understand half steps and *whole steps*. As you learned on page 13, a half step is the distance between two notes that are one fret apart. For example, the distance between the 1st and 2nd frets is a half step. A whole step is the distance between two notes that are two frets apart (have one fret between them). For example, the distance between the 1st and 3rd frets is a whole step.

Major Scale Construction

1. The major scale has seven different notes.

2. The eighth note is the same as the first note but an octave (eight steps through the musical alphabet) higher.

3. The formula for creating the major scale is a specific arrangement of whole steps (W) and half steps (H): W–W–H–W–W–W–H.

Below is a C Major scale. Starting on the note C, we go up a whole step to D, then a whole step to E, then a half step to F, and so on. The first note, C, is called the *tonic* or *key note*. It is helpful to give each note in the scale a number.

C Major Scale

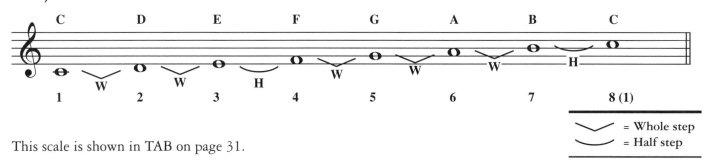

This scale is shown in TAB on page 31.

Let's take the major scale formula and apply it to the pedal steel guitar. Because the pedal steel is tuned to an E Major chord, we will begin with the E Major scale, which can be played on open strings.

Notice that you will be using both the A and B pedals in this scale. There will be some new notes so study this example carefully, playing the scale many times.

E Major Scale

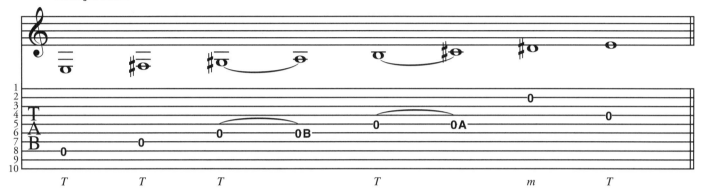

G Major is another commonly used major scale. Notice that it has no open strings. Again, study this scale carefully, repeating it many times. You need to become very comfortable with reading and playing all of these notes.

G Major Scale

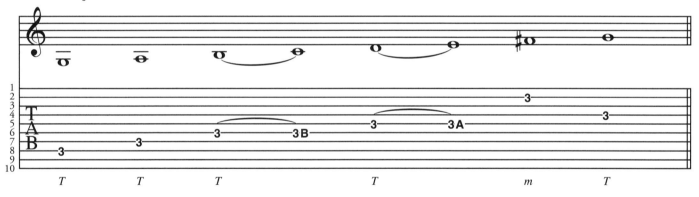

Keys

Notice that applying the major scale formula to a scale starting on the note G results in a scale with one sharp: F♯. These notes comprise the key of G Major. When playing a song that has these notes, you are very likely playing in the key of G Major.

Notice that the C Major scale on page 31 has all natural notes. When playing a song with all natural notes, it is quite likely that you are playing in the key of C Major. This very important information is just the tip of the iceberg; there's a lot more to know. But this understanding gets you started down the road to being a real musician!

The major scale formula of whole steps and half steps can be used to figure out other major scales. If you know where the notes are on your guitar, you can play in any key. This will become helpful when playing songs with other musicians. You can use the handy fretboard chart on page 17 as a reference.

Key Signatures

A *key signature* is a group of sharps or flats that appear at the beginning of a staff and indicate the key. For example, one sharp (F#) in the key signature indicates the key of G Major.

Key signature

TRIADS

A *chord* is a group of three or more notes played together, like the string groups on pages 38–41. A *triad* is a certain type of three-note chord constructed by stacking every other note of a scale. Below, a *G Major triad* (chord symbol: G) is built from a G Major scale.

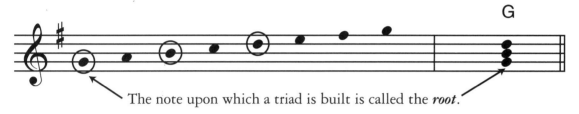

The note upon which a triad is built is called the *root*.

After the root, the other notes in the triad are called the 3rd and 5th because of their positions in the scale from which they were derived.

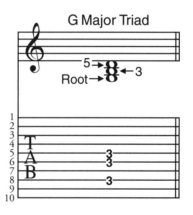

G Major Triad

We can create a triad on every note of the major scale. Universally, musicians number these triads with Roman numerals. Just in case you're not familiar with Roman numerals, their Arabic equivalents are shown below. The three most important chords in any key are I, IV and V.

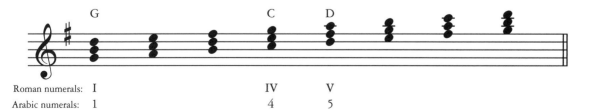

Roman numerals: I   IV   V
Arabic numerals: 1   4   5

Dotted Notes

Placing a *dot* to the right of a note increases its value by half. A *dotted half note* is worth three beats. You can think of a dotted half note as being equal to a half note tied to a quarter note.

Dotted Half Note

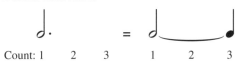

Count: 1   2   3   1   2   3

The following song, "Goodnight Ladies," uses string groups to play the melody in *block chord style*, which means that the melody note is played on the top of the chord. Notice that we move up to the 10th fret for the D Major chord in the fourth measure and to the 8th fret for the C Major chord in the sixth measure.

Goodnight Ladies   Track 21

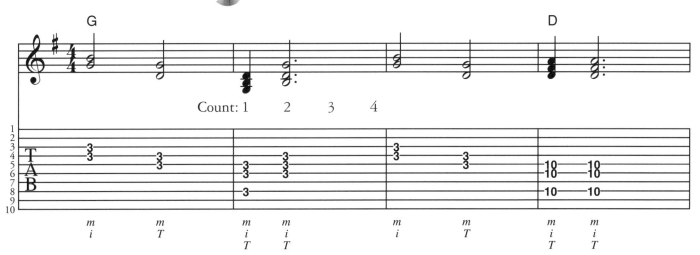

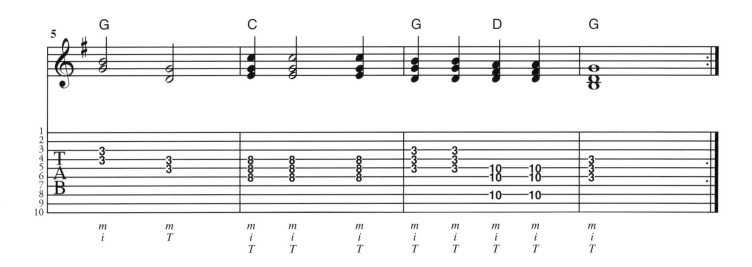

USING THE A PEDAL

We will begin with the A pedal. This is the pedal on the left side. It raises the 5th and 10th strings one whole step. **See the photo below for the correct foot placement.**

If you didn't tune the pedals in the tuning section, or if they don't sound quite right, refer back to page 15 for step-by-step instructions.

New Note with the A Pedal: C♯

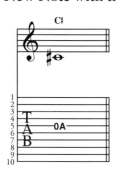

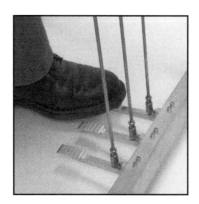

This is a short example for you to play and get used to your foot placement.

The pedal will be notated with a capital A after the TAB number.

You learned about slurred notes on page 20. As you will recall, the second note in a slur is not picked. Here is an exercise for practicing slurred pedal notes.

A Pedal Exercise 1   **Track 22**

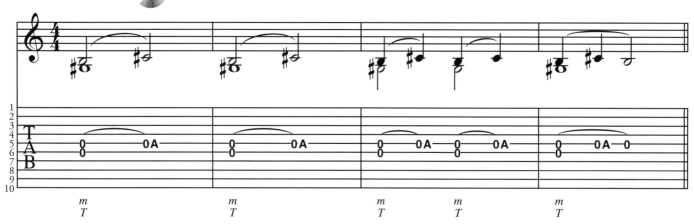

Remember, there are two ways to play notes that use the pedals, attacked and slurred. To play an attacked pedal note, pick the pedaled note with your right hand.

A Pedal Exercise 2 Track 23

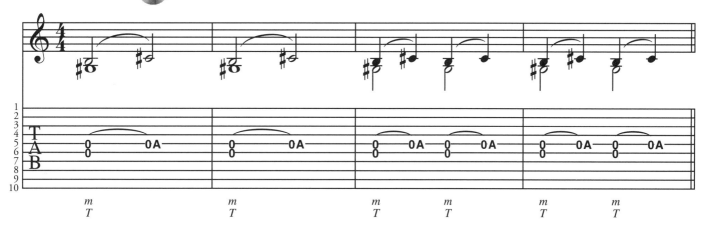

 MINI MUSIC LESSON

Eighth Notes and Rests

An *eighth note* is equal to one half of a quarter note. It is half a beat in duration, so two eighth notes equal one quarter note. A single eighth note looks like a quarter note but has an added flag. Two or more consecutive eighth notes are connected with a beam.

Count eighth notes by saying "1-&, 2-&, 3-&, 4-&," etc. As you tap your foot, the "&" part of the beat is when your foot is up off the ground.

Eighth Rest

An *eighth rest* indicates half a beat of silence.

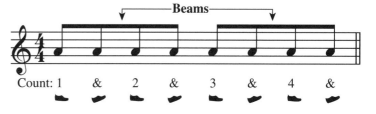

Eighth Note Exercise Track 24

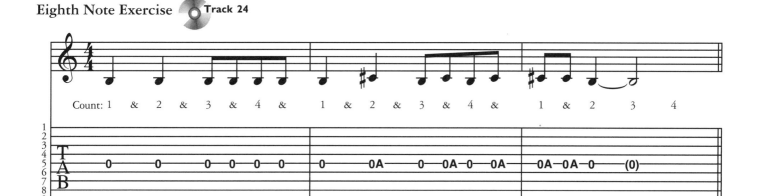

New Notes:
Many of the examples that follow will make use of double stops at new locations on the neck.

Here are notes used in double stops at the 3rd, 8th and 10th frets.

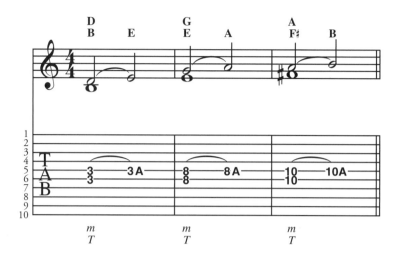

Notice that in A Pedal Exercise 3 below, we use the steel on the 3rd, 8th and 10th frets. You will also notice that even though we might be playing only two notes at one time, these notes are from the 4–5–6 string group.

A Pedal Exercise 3   **Track 25**

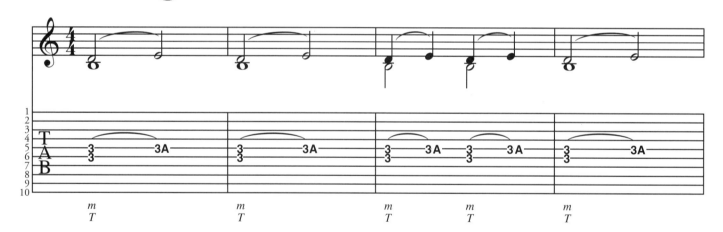

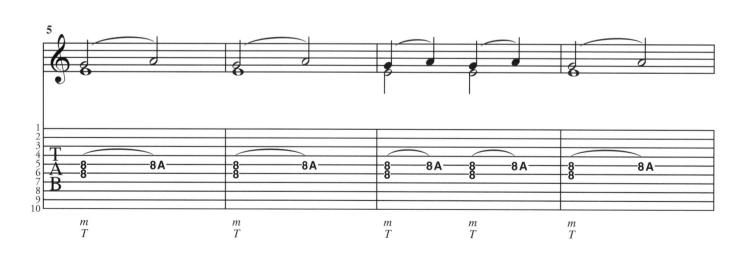

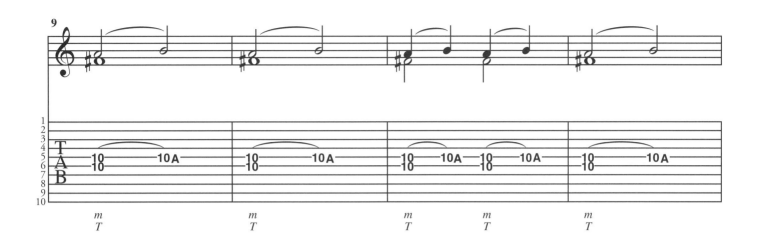

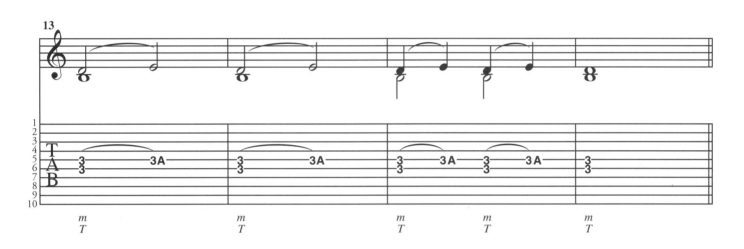

Nominated to the Steel Guitar Hall of Fame in 1985, **Curly Chalker** is known as the "King of Chords." Known for his work on the C6 neck, he is a master of both the E9 and C6 necks of the pedal steel guitar. Chalker has a very distinctive sound, with his use of percussive chordal attacks, volume swells and *gutting*, which is a technique of attacking a note or chord and quickly rolling off the volume pedal and bringing it back on. As his reputation grew in the 1960s, Chalker moved from Las Vegas to Nashville and became one of the most in-demand session players.

Notice that the A pedal is used to play the melody notes in this holiday favorite while the chords are played without the pedals.

The Dotted Quarter Note
As you learned on page 45, placing a dot to the right of a note increases its value by half. A dotted quarter note is worth one-and-one-half (1½) beats. You can think of a dotted quarter note as being equal to a quarter note tied to an eighth note.

Count: 1   &   2   =   1   &   2

Silent Night Track 26

Solemnly

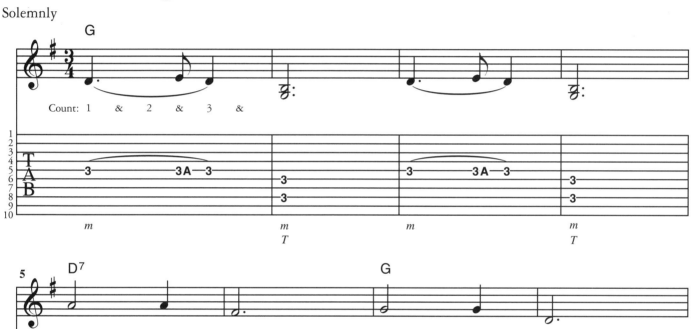

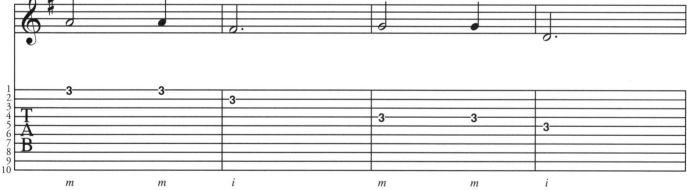

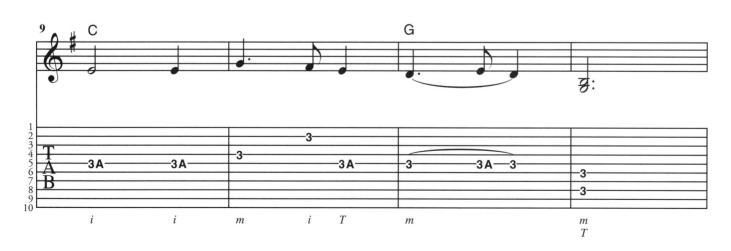

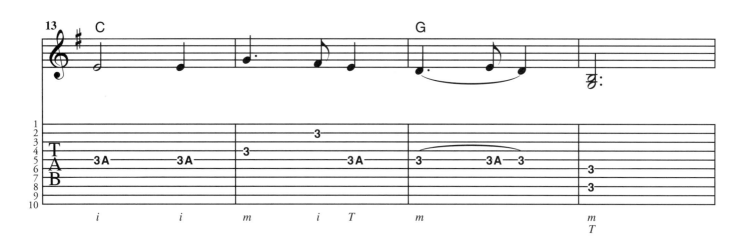

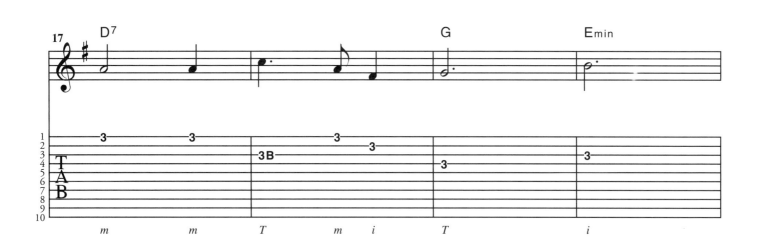

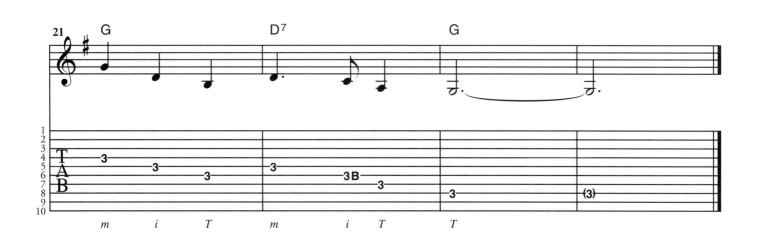

USING THE B PEDAL

The B pedal is the center pedal. It raises the 3rd and 6th strings one half step.

New Note with the B Pedal: A

B Pedal Exercise 1 will help you get used to the foot placement and sound of playing with this pedal.

B Pedal Exercise 1 Track 27

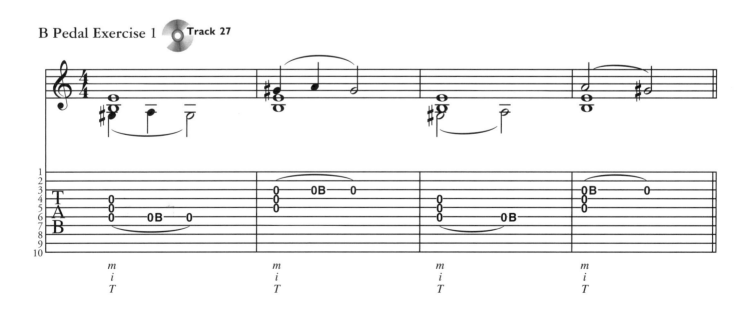

The next example uses the B pedal to change the bottom note in a chord. Note that although we move up to the 8th and 10th frets rather quickly, the pattern is the same until the last two measures, where there is a big slide from the 10th to the 15th fret (which is the same as the 3rd fret but an octave higher).

B Pedal Exercise 2   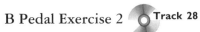 **Track 28**

We begin learning this classic country song in the *open position* (the steel is not used). The purpose is to coordinate your right hand with the pedal, and concentrate on the pedal movement. Practice this slowly and gradually speed up as you are able. Be careful to mute the strings so as not to let the notes run into each other.

Bury Me Beneath the Willow (Open Position) Track 29

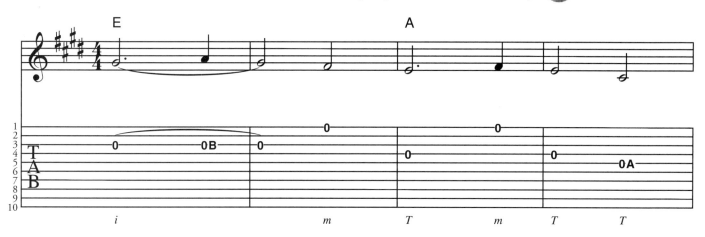

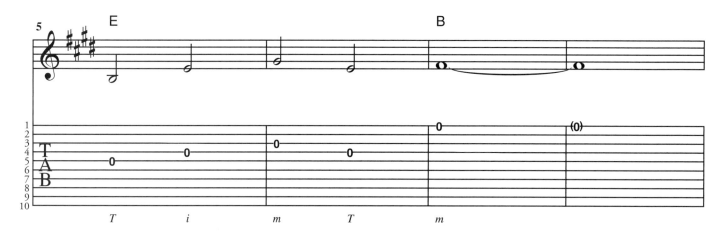

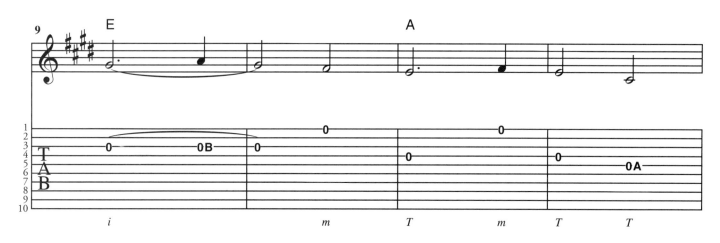

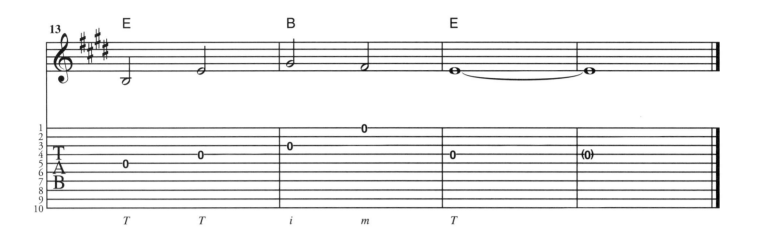

HELPFUL HINT

Bar Following

Bar following is a technique used in playing the pedal steel where you move the steel (often called the *bar*) back and forth across the strings keeping the tip near the top string you are playing. This accomplishes two things:

1) You are able to see better where the steel is placed over the fret because more of the fret is visible, and

2) It helps you to better mute the unplayed strings, in this case, with your right hand.

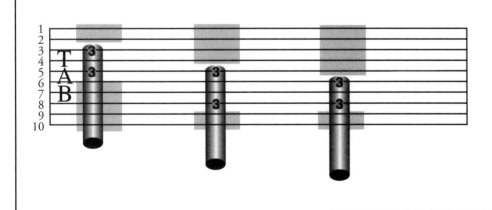

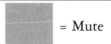 = Mute

PUTTING THE A AND B PEDALS TOGETHER

The A and B pedals can be combined to create a "country" sound. This is especially useful when playing chordal arrangements of songs. When both the A and B pedals are depressed simultaneously (see photo for foot placement), the sound of the existing chord is raised a *perfect 4th* (a distance of five half steps). This would be the same as moving from a C chord to an F chord, or from an E to an A chord.

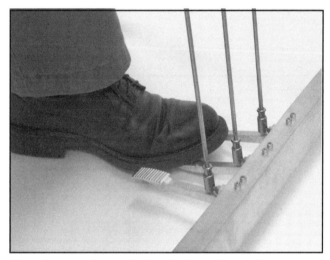

Foot placement for combining the A and B pedals.

A and B Pedal Exercise 1   Track 30

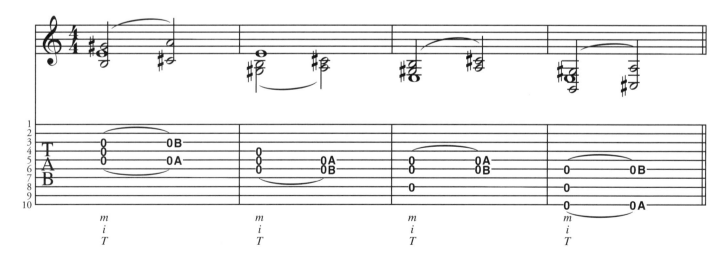

Play the next example slowly at first and be sure that both pedals are depressed all the way to keep the chords in tune.

A and B Pedal Exercise 2   Track 31

"Long Journey Home" uses the A
and B pedals together. Staying
within two string groups (3–4–5 and
4–5–6), it has a big, 12 fret slide at
the end.

Long Journey Home Track 32

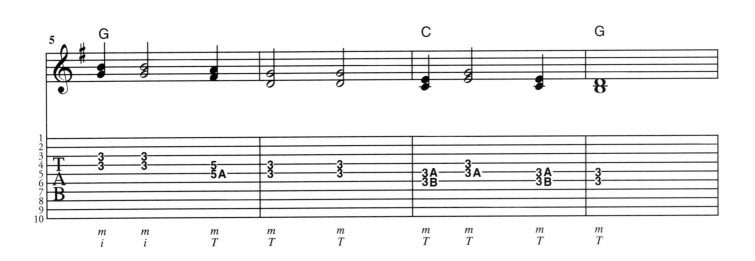

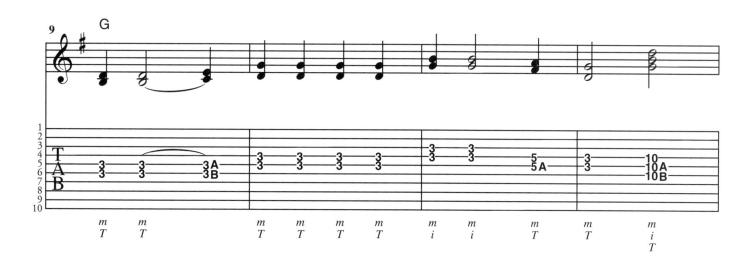

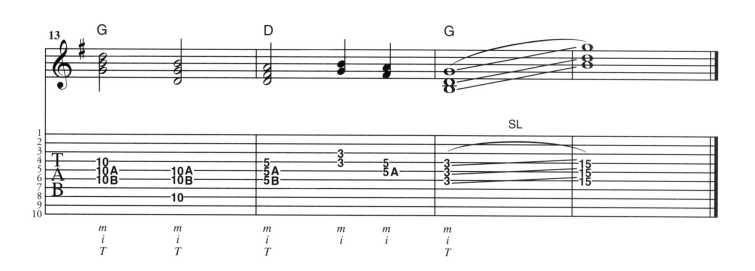

Doug Jernigan is one of the great pedal steel guitar players of his generation. He is one of the first steel players to perfect the technique of playing single notes very quickly, keeping up with banjo and fiddle players. He spent a lot of time on the road perfecting his skills behind the likes of Vasser Clements, Faron Young and Jimmy Dickens as well as becoming one of the most sought-after pedal steel guitarists for recording sessions.

Doug has also become an educator and promoter of the steel guitar, authoring a number of instructional books and video courses.

Not limiting himself to country music, Doug is also a fine jazz player and has recorded a number of great jazz albums. He was inducted into the Steel Guitar Hall of Fame in 1994.

Buddy Emmons is known as the foremost steel guitar player in the business. In 1963, he recorded the landmark album, *Steel Guitar Jazz* and began a five year stint with Ray Price and his Cherokee Cowboys. In 1965 he teamed up with fellow steel player Shot Jackson to record the album, *Steel Guitar & Dobro Sound*. This led the two to create the Sho-Bud Company, and together they developed the pedal steel guitar that we know today.

PHOTO BY CLAY SAVAGE • COURTESY OF TOM BRADSHAW

The next song, "Bury Me Beneath the Willow," is the same song you learned on page 54 but this time it makes use of the A and B pedals together and moves through the different string groups. Notice the slide in measures 8 and 9 and also measures 15 and 16. This technique is used to make a phrase ending with long notes more interesting.

Bury Me Beneath the Willow Track 33

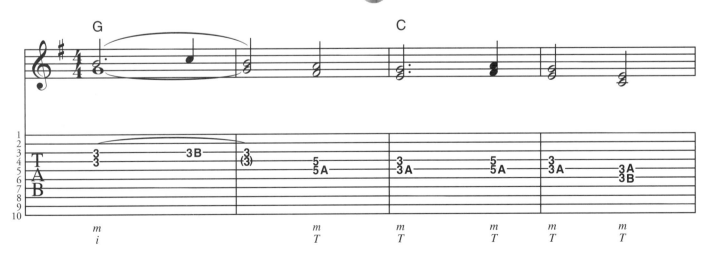

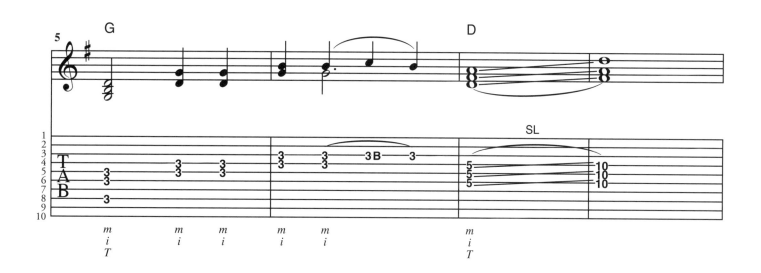

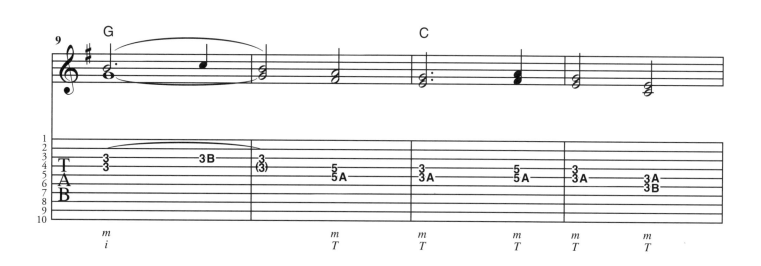

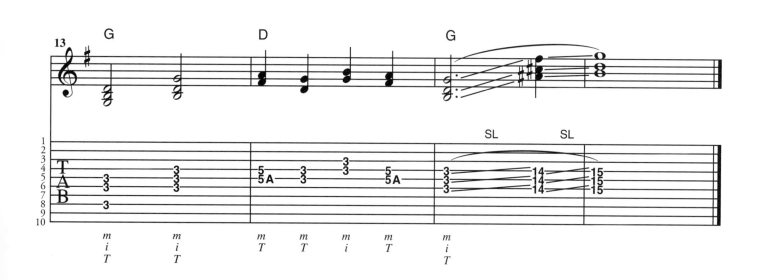

USING THE VOLUME PEDAL

By now you have probably been starting to use the volume pedal a little. The most common uses for the volume pedal are to sustain notes and to alter the attack of notes and chords. The key to good volume pedal technique is not to over use it; use it in a way that adds to the music.

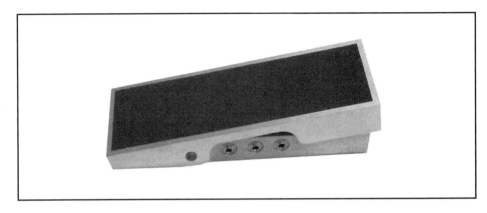

To use the volume pedal correctly, depress the pedal about halfway with your right foot. This will be the normal setting for the pedal. Next adjust the volume on your amplifier to suit your needs and taste.

When the volume on your amplifier is set, play a chord on your guitar. Notice that the sound of the chord fades away after a short time. As the chord you play begins to fade away, slowly depress the volume pedal so that the volume of the chord remains constant until the pedal is fully depressed. The idea is to improve your *sustain*.

Volume Pedal Example 1: Sustain Track 34

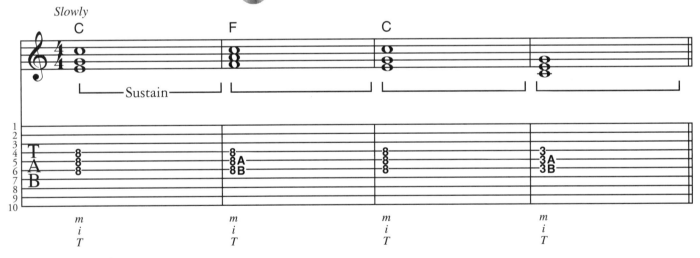

The other major use of the volume pedal is to alter the attack of a note or chord by using a volume *swell*. To swell, attack a note or chord on the guitar with the volume pedal turned off and then slowly depress the pedal, allowing the chord or note to be heard. This technique is very effective when used sparingly.

 MINI MUSIC LESSON

Crescendo and Decrescendo
Crescendo (kreh-SHEN-doh) means to gradually become louder. This is what happens in a volume swell. The musical symbol for a crescendo is:

Decrescendo (deh-kreh-SHEN-doh) means to gradually become quieter. The musical symbol for a decrescendo is:

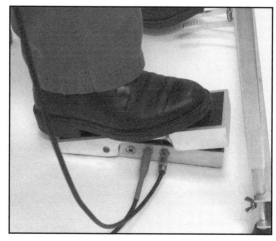

Pedal off

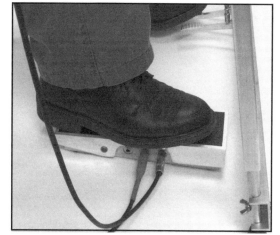

Pedal on

Volume Pedal Example 2: Swells   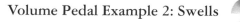 Track 35

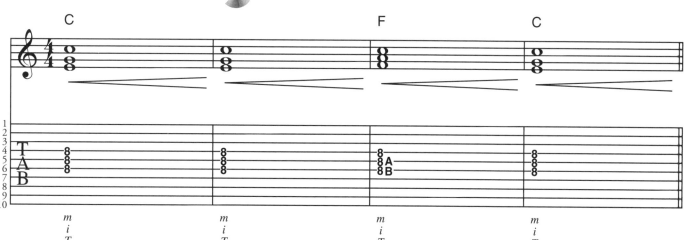

Volume Pedal Example 3   Track 36

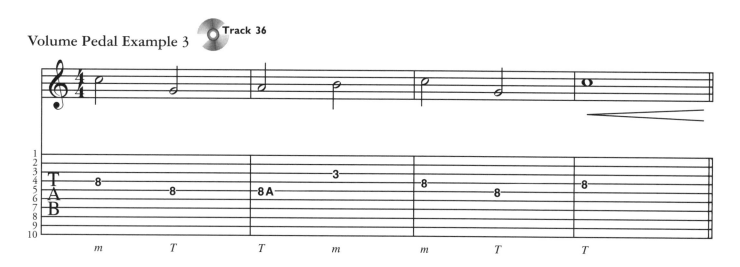

Volume pedal techniques are a standard part of the pedal steel guitar sound, and are not necessarily written into the music. Use them at your discretion, but sparingly!

Here are some fun tunes to play. Enjoy!

Roll On Buddy Track 37

Dark Hollow

 Track 38

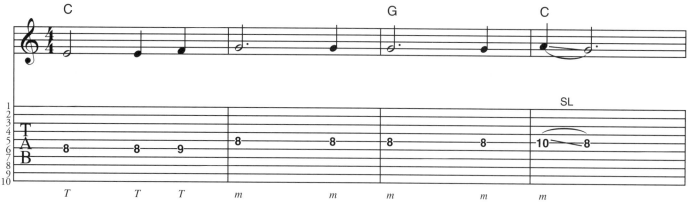

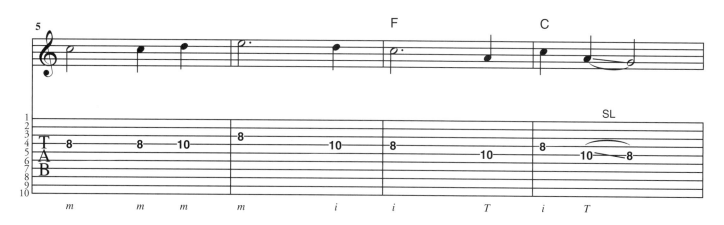

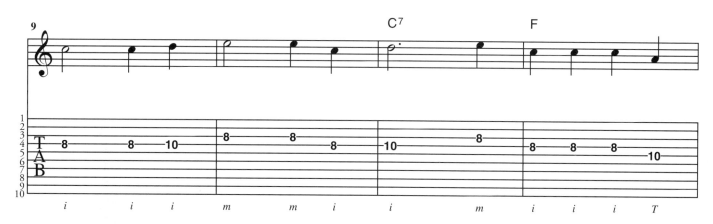

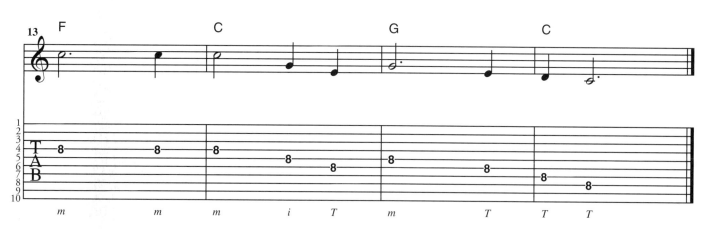

This one uses the C Major scale and both the A and B pedals.

Scaling the Bar   Track 39

Harmonized Scales

Harmony is the sound of two or more notes played together. A *harmonized scale* is a scale with additional notes stacked above or below the scale tones. When these additional notes are scale tones themselves, it is called *diatonic harmony*. Here is the harmonized C Major scale.

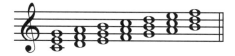

Harmonized scales can be used to create your own licks or to spice up a melody. When practicing harmonized scales, learn them starting on the first note of the scale (the tonic) and also starting on different scale tones.

The following examples harmonize the C Major scale mostly with notes an *interval* of a *3rd* below. An interval is the distance between two notes, and a 3rd is a distance of either three or four half steps.

Harmonized Scale Example 1 stays primarily at the 1st and 3rd frets.

Harmonized Scale Example 1   Track 40

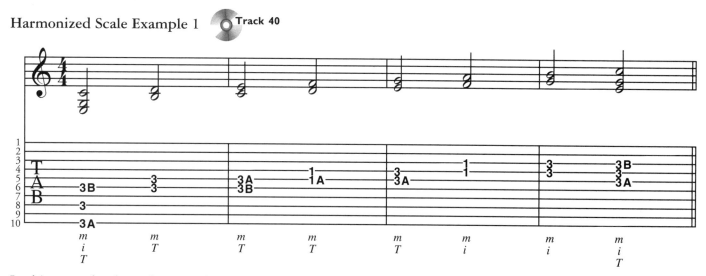

In this example, the scale moves in a more linear fashion up the fretboard, from the 3rd fret to the 10th fret on the 5th and 6th strings.

Harmonized Scale Example 2   Track 41

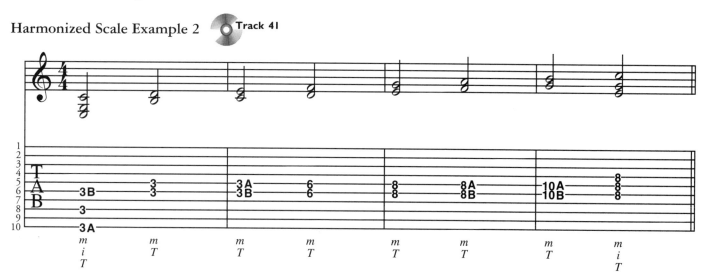

Pickups and Incomplete Measures

Notice that the first measure of "Amazing Grace" has only one note. This note is called a *pickup* note or measure. Pickup notes come before the first full measure and are used to lead into a song. When a song begins with a pickup measure, it ends with an *incomplete measure* to make up for the additional beat(s) at the beginning. When in $\frac{4}{4}$ time, if the pickup measure has one beat, the incomplete measure at the end will have three beats. In "Amazing Grace," which is in $\frac{3}{4}$ time and has a one-beat pickup, the incomplete measure at the end has two beats. Here are the pickup and incomplete measures from "Amazing Grace."

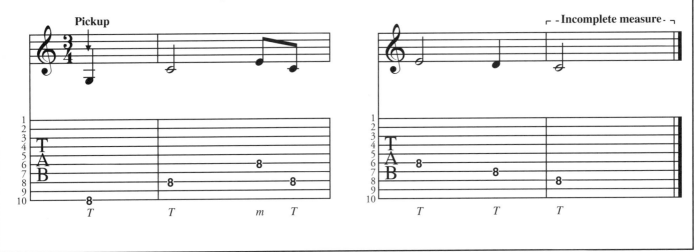

Amazing Grace   Track 42

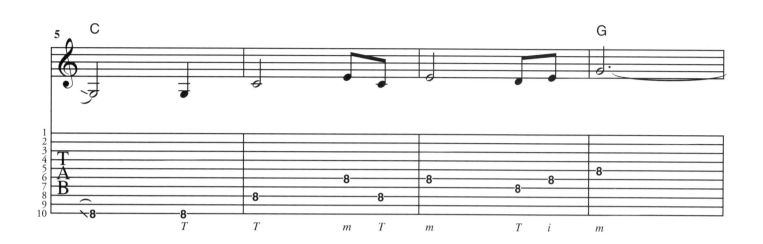

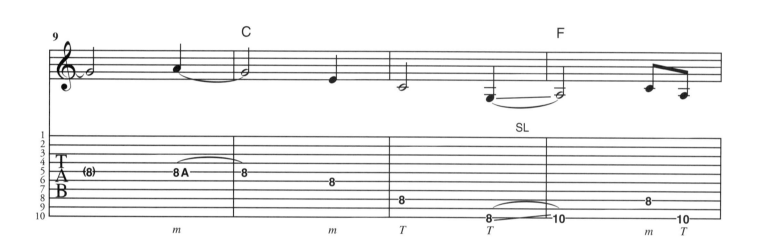

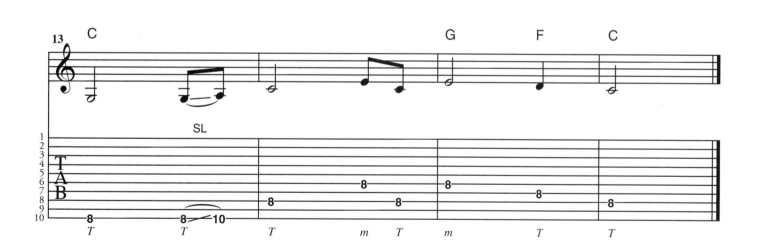

INTRODUCTIONS

As the pedal steel player in a band, you will often be called upon to supply an introduction, or intro, to a song. This is simply a short phrase of one or more measures to lead the band into the song. Your options here are limitless and the next few examples will get you started.

This first intro begins on the V (G7) chord (7th chords will be covered on page 78) and resolves to the I chord (C) of the song.

Introduction Example 1   Track 43

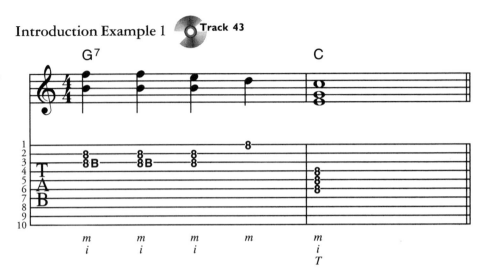

Introduction Example 2 also begins on the V chord (G) but uses a C Major scale beginning on the G as a way to arrive at the I (C) chord. Play slowly at first—the pedal changes can be a little tricky.

Introduction Example 2   Track 44

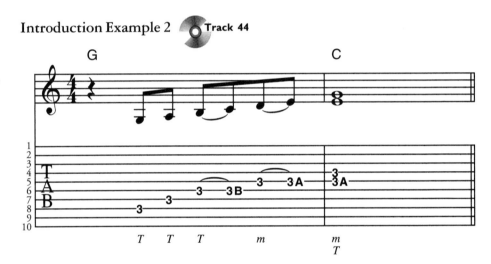

This intro is a little more complicated; it has slides as well as pedal moves. Proceed slowly!

Introduction Example 3   Track 45

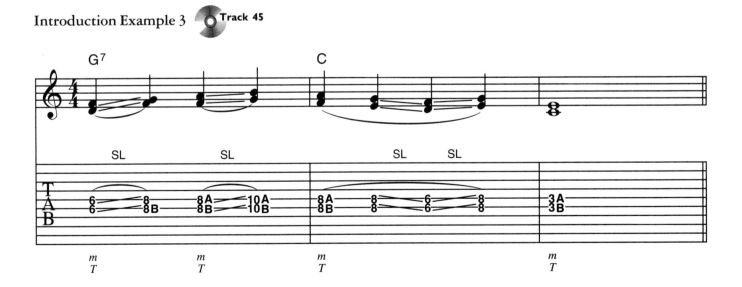

This example uses three different string groups and will sound great on a *ballad* (slow song).

Introduction Example 4   Track 46

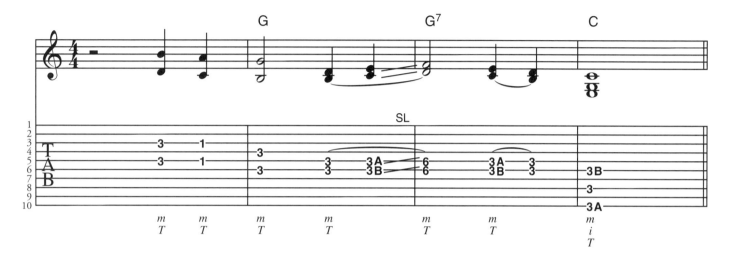

This final introduction example will take some practice. Try breaking it up into small sections and then put it together. Listen to the recorded example to hear the pedal moves. The A pedal should be applied slowly while holding down the B pedal to achieve the characteristic "crying" sound. Try this one in different places on the neck.

Introduction Example 5   Track 47

ENDINGS

The pedal steel player often supplies the *ending* lick or phrase to a country song. This phrase is often short, a measure or two, and adds the final *cadence* (the harmonic close of a section or song) usually from a V chord to a I chord.

It is important that you know a few ending licks in the common keys. The following examples will be in the key of G Major, but you can *transpose* (change the key) in most cases simply by moving your bar up or down to the desired fret. For example, notice that Ending

Example 1, in G Major, is mostly built around the G on the 3rd fret of the 3rd string. If you move it up two frets, a whole step, to the A on the 5th fret, the lick will be in the key of A Major. The last chord will also be two frets higher. Try it!

This example is in the key of C Major and played at the 8th fret.

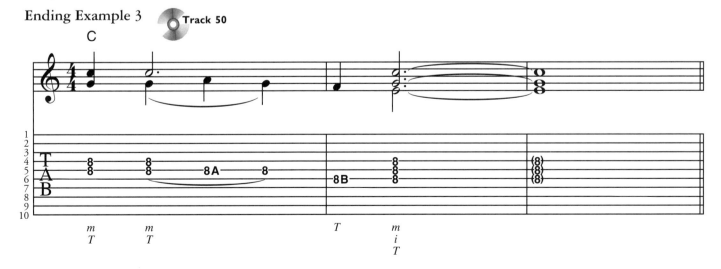

Ending Example 4 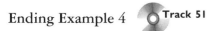 **Track 51**

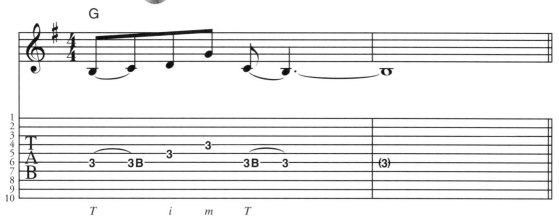

This ending is a *cascading* scale passage. In a cascading scale, adjacent notes are played on different strings and ring through one another, creating a harp-like sound. Let each note ring out. The right-hand fingering is a bit tricky, so learn it slowly.

Ending Example 5 **Track 52**

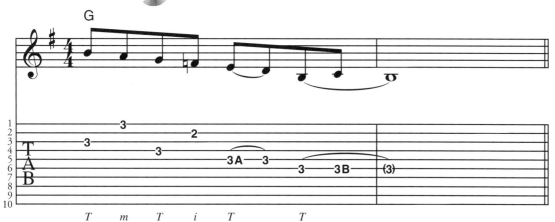

This is an ending in the style of Buck Owens. Notice that we are playing at the 15th fret, which is one octave higher than the 3rd fret. You could play the same passage at the 3rd fret and still be in the key of G.

HELPFUL HINT The guitar fretboard "starts over" again at the 12th fret. When playing on these upper frets, think of the 12th fret as being like the open strings and count up from there.

Ending Example 6 **Track 53**

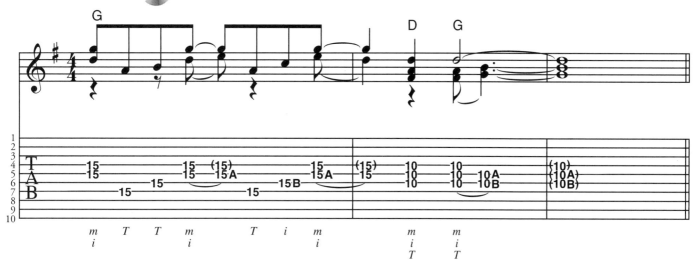

This arrangement of the song "Will the Circle Be Unbroken" uses both an introduction and an ending. The double bar at bar 3 is used to separate the introduction and the beginning of the melody.

Will the Circle Be Unbroken Track 54

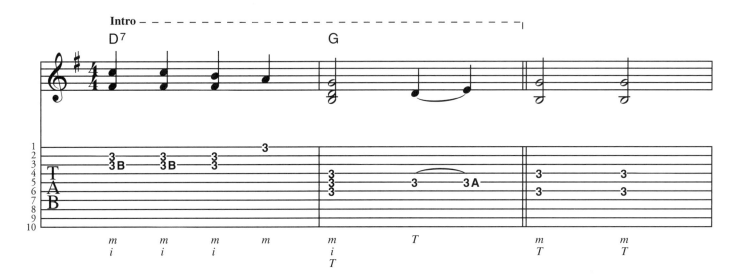

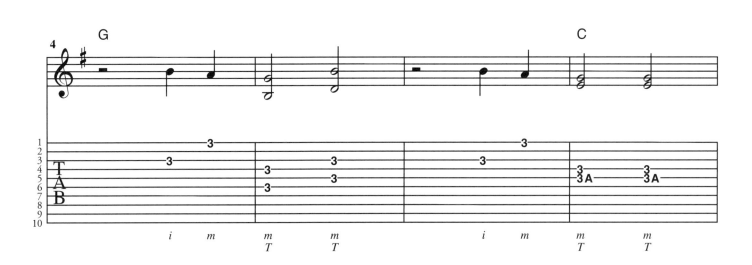

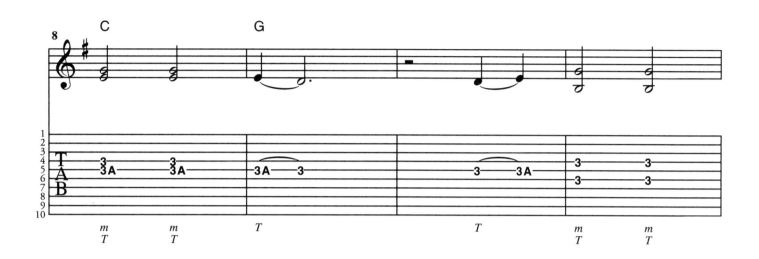

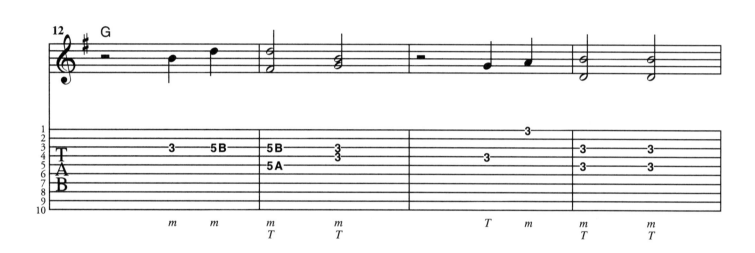

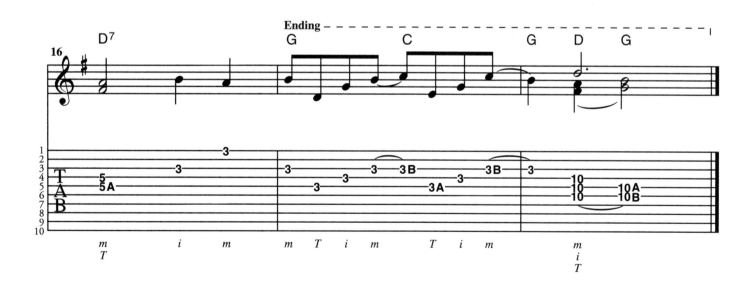

1st and 2nd Endings

MINI MUSIC LESSON

1st and 2nd endings are a way of showing that the same section of music is to be repeated but has a different ending the second time. When you get to the repeat sign, go back and play that section again and when you get to the 1st ending, skip it and play the 2nd ending instead.

Precious Memories   Track 55

Slowly

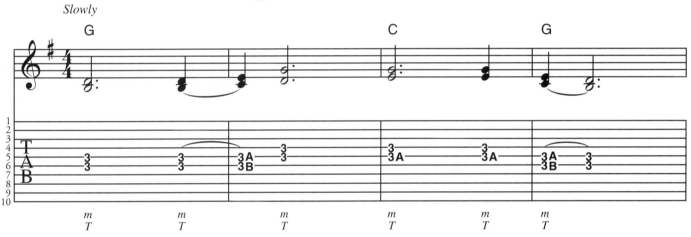

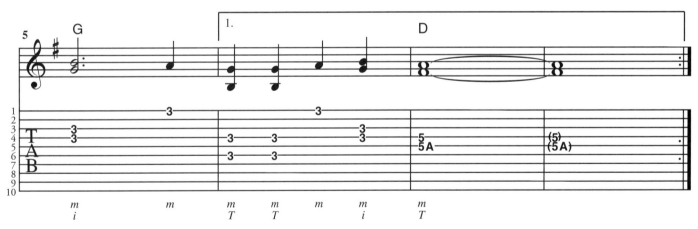

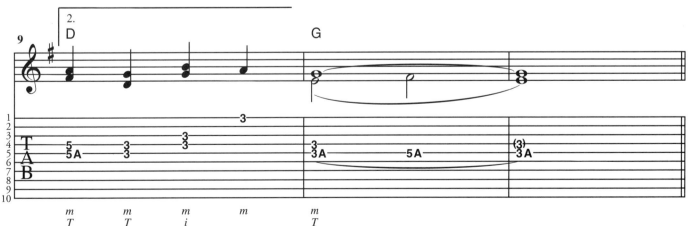

THE E KNEE LEVER

The E knee lever is, for the most part, used more than any of the other knee levers on the pedal steel. While there is no standard number of knee levers on the pedal steel, the E knee lever is on just about every model including most entry-level pedal steel guitars. The E knee lever lowers the 4th and 8th strings, both E strings, to E♭. This change greatly enhances the steel guitar, allowing you to play more types of chords without jumping up and down the neck. These additional chord types are: dominant 7th, major 7th and minor chords. Let's take a look at these chords beginning with the dominant 7th chord.

Dominant 7th Chords

A dominant 7th chord (chord symbol: 7) is a major triad with an additional note added a *minor 3rd* (a distance of three half steps) above the 5th, creating a four-note chord. The added note is called a ♭7 (flat-7), and is the seventh degree of the scale lowered one half step. There is a major 3rd interval (four half steps) between the root and 3rd, a minor 3rd between the 3rd and 5th and a minor 3rd between the 5th and 7th.

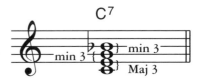

This example shows three ways to play a dominant 7th chord, in this case, G7.

Dominant 7th Chord Example 1   Track 56

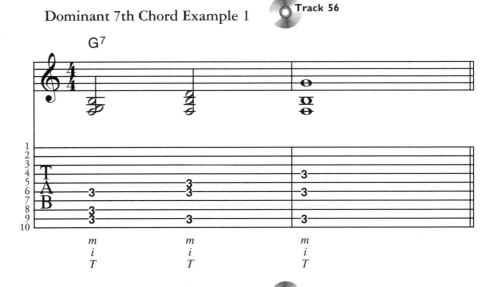

Another way to play dominant 7th chords is to use the E knee lever together with the B pedal. With this combination, you can play 7th chords on the I, IV and V chords in one position.

Dominant 7th Chord Example 2   Track 57

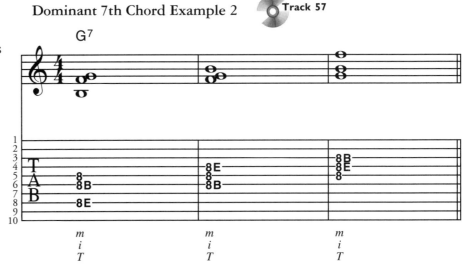

This example is in C Major. Take a look at how the I (C) and V (G7) chords work together in the same position.

Dominant 7th Chord Example 3 Track 58

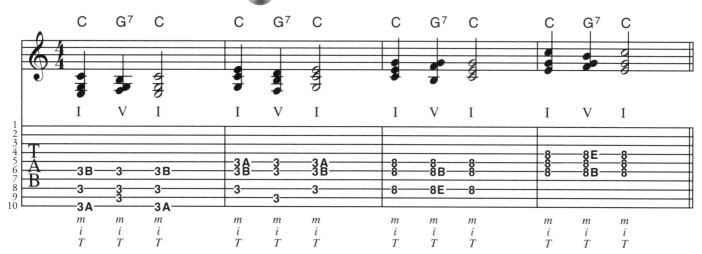

Minor Triads

A *minor triad* (chord symbol: min) has a minor 3rd interval between the root and 3rd and a major 3rd between the 3rd and 5th.

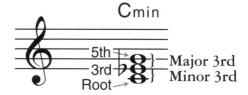

You can create a minor triad by lowering the 3rd of a major triad, thus creating a chord formula of root–♭3–5. Here's the G Minor triad created by lowering the 3rd of a G Major triad.

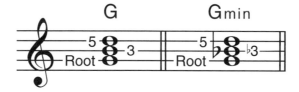

Chord Inversions

A *chord inversion* is a chord whose lowest tone is something other than the root. A *1st inversion* chord has the 3rd in the bass and a *2nd inversion* chord has the 5th in the bass.

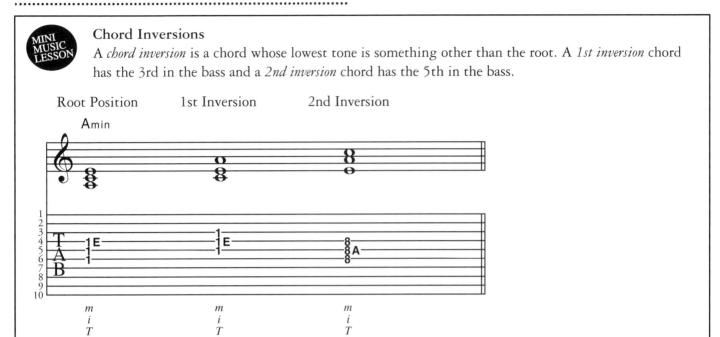

In this next example, you will play different inversions of the A Minor chord at the 1st, 3rd and 8th frets.

Inversion Example 1   Track 59

Inversion Example 2   Track 60

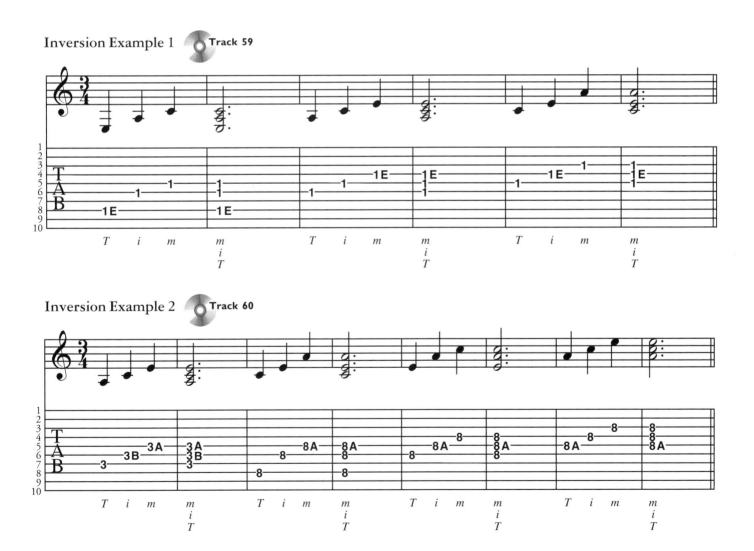

THE C PEDAL

The C pedal, in combination with the B pedal, can also be used to create minor chords one whole step above a major chord (no pedal) at the same fret.

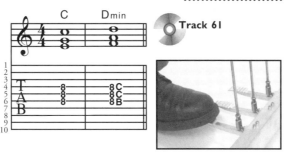

"Moving Forward" is played entirely at the 8th fret and uses major, minor and dominant 7th chords. Notice the use of the C pedal in bar 5. Work it out slowly, being careful to mute unwanted strings. Bar 15 has a pedal slur through the first three chords. This is a common technique that can be used in ballads.

Moving Forward

THE BLUES

The influence of the blues is universal. It is a language that just about every musician can speak. The blues form can be found in musical styles ranging from rock, country, bluegrass and to jazz and many others.

In performing the blues, a musician is able to express the range of human emotions, from playful and witty, thoughtful to deeply sad and somber.

Learning the blues form and language is an essential part of becoming a well-rounded musician.

Here's a brief summary of the blues form:

- Usually 12 measures in length. This form is often called the *12-bar blues*.

- The most basic form of the blues uses just three chords.

- The chord changes occur at specific points regardless of the style of music.

The following example shows the basic 12-bar blues form in the key of G Major. Note that the chords change at bars 5, 7, 9, 10 and 11.

This is a blues in G. The pitches are written 8vb, which means that they sound an octave lower than written. This is done to make the music easier to read.

Blues in G   Track 63

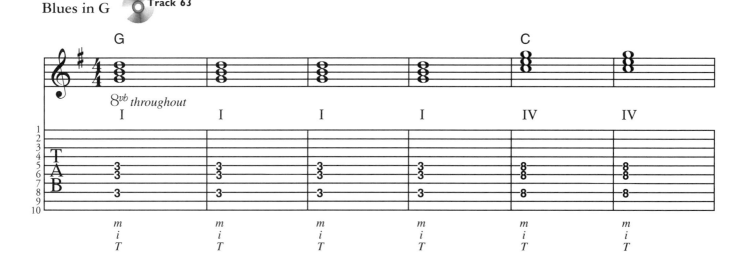

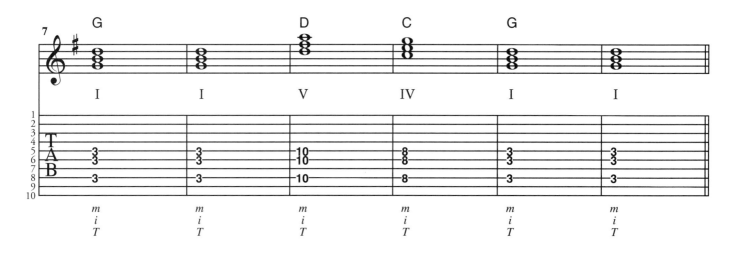

This is a blues in E.

Seventh Degree Blues Track 64

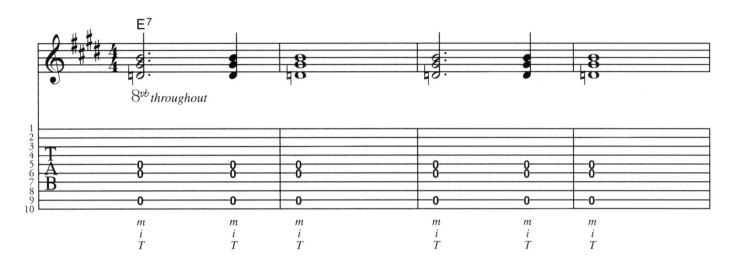

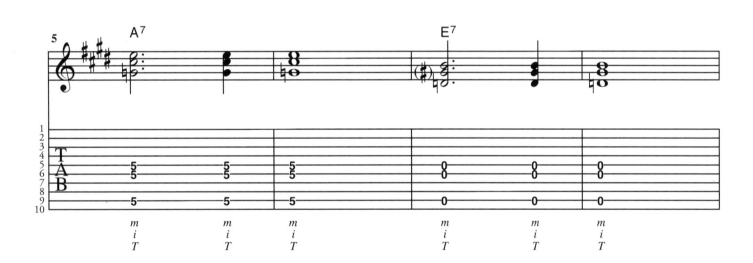

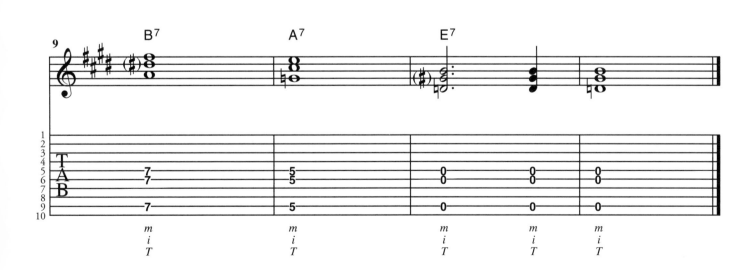

HELPFUL HINT

This is the lick on which the next song, "A Pedal Blues," is based. Notice that the A pedal remains depressed for most of the lick. Practice it slowly at first to develop the proper timing with the A pedal. After you learn it in the open position, simply transfer to other keys by placing your bar over the desired fret.

The second half of the song has the same lick played an octave higher. The lick now begins on the 5th string. Notice that the fourth note jumps to the 1st string. Again, practice it slowly as the picking pattern can be tricky.

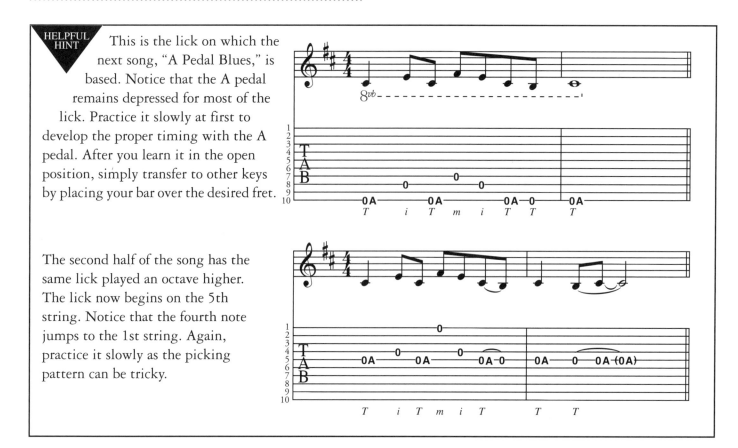

A Pedal Blues   Track 65

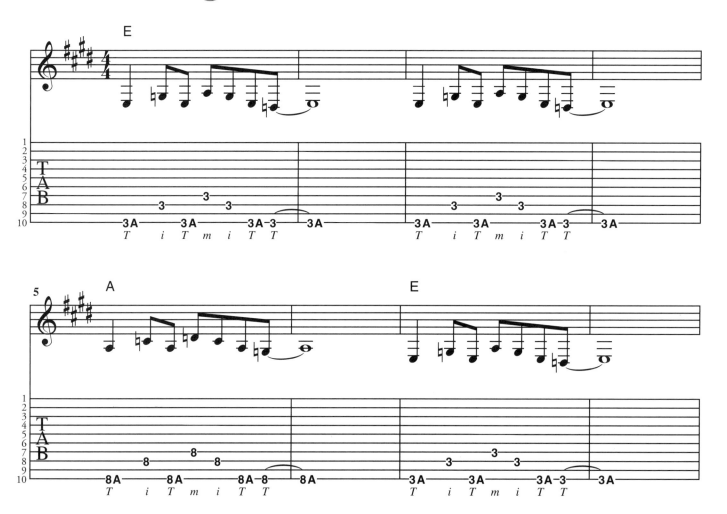

Blues Soloing

It's time to start thinking about improvisation. This section will teach you the scales needed to play blues solos.

In addition to the major scale, the most important scales to use in playing the blues are the *major pentatonic* and *minor pentatonic* scales. It is very easy to learn these scales because they have a lot in common.

Major Pentatonic Scale and Licks

The major pentatonic scale has a happy sound and is widely used in bluegrass and country music. This scale uses the first, second, third, fifth and sixth notes of the major scale (1–2–3–5–6). It's that simple.

Here's what the major pentatonic scale looks like in the key of G.

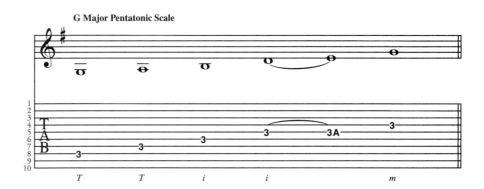

One effective way to begin learning how to solo is to learn short musical ideas called *licks*. Ultimately, you'll string them together to create solos.

Major Pentatonic Scale Example 1   Track 66

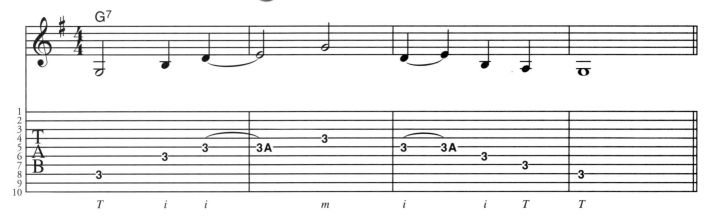

Play through this one slowly at first, making sure that the unwanted strings are muted.

Major Pentatonic Scale Example 2   **Track 67**

Minor Pentatonic Scale

The minor pentatonic scale is probably the most widely-used scale for blues, country and rock. To derive this scale from the major scale, we must lower some of the notes one half step. The minor pentatonic scale uses the first, lowered-third, fourth, fifth and flatted-seventh ($1-\flat 3-4-5-\flat 7$) of the major scale.

Here's what the minor pentatonic scale looks like written in the key of C.

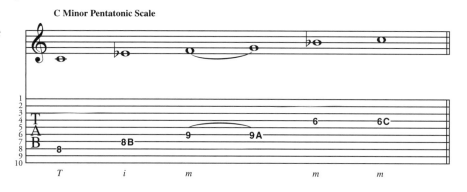

Pedal Steel Licks

Here's a few fun licks to give you some ideas for making up your own solos.

This first lick uses the major scale position at the 3rd fret. Listen to the CD to hear how to phrase the A pedal in the second measure. The A pedal should be applied slowly but in tempo to achieve the characteristic steel guitar sound.

Lick 1   Track 68

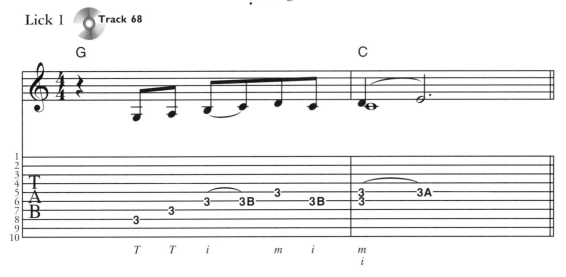

> **HELPFUL HINT** Using a metronome will help you keep a steady beat while learning these licks. As you count into the examples, keep in mind that the first beats are silent.

The next phrase begins on the second half of the first beat. Be careful in the second measure, as it can be a little tricky for the A pedal.

Lick 2   Track 69

This next example is a variation on
Lick 1 on page 88.

Lick 3 Track 70

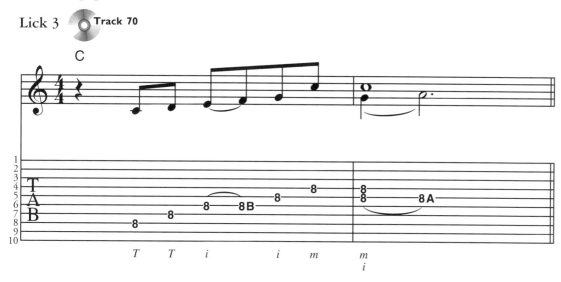

As in Lick 3, Lick 4 begins on the
second beat.

Lick 4 Track 71

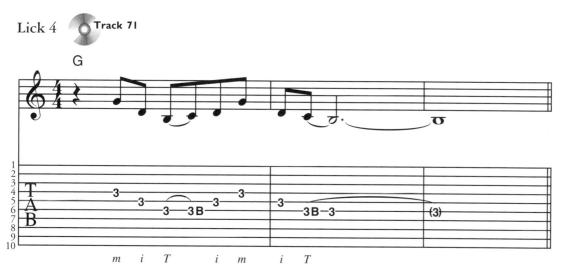

Speedy West

Perhaps one of our most flamboyant pedal steel guitarists ever, **Speedy West** is one of the pioneers of the pedal steel guitar. Best known for his work with Jimmy Bryant, he also recorded several best-selling hits with Tennessee Ernie Ford and Kay Starr. Speedy developed tunings and many techniques that gave his sound additional expression. He had an aggressive approach to the steel guitar that was the perfect compliment to Jimmy Bryant's smooth technique. Together they recorded several records for Capital Records and played on numerous sessions for other artists. Speedy was inducted into the Steel Guitar Hall of Fame in 1980.

"Worried Man Blues" is a traditional song in the blues and country style. It is fun to play and contains some tricky picking. It is in the open position (key of E) so you can concentrate on the right-hand picking and the left foot on the pedals.

HELPFUL HINT When there is a pedal change from playing both the A and B pedals to the A pedal only as in bars 5 and 6, keep both pedals pressed down because you may need the B pedal afterwards, as in bar 7, and this makes for a smoother transition.

Worried Man Blues Track 72

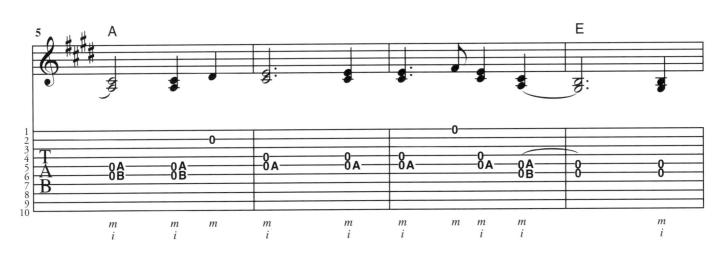

TRIPLETS

A *triplet* is three notes played in the time of two. For example, three eighth notes played in the time of two, or three eighth notes per beat, make an *eighth-note triplet*. Notice that triplet eighth notes are beamed in groups of three and are labeled with the number 3. Because we are now dividing the beat into three equal parts, we must count differently.

Count: 1   &   ah   2   &   ah   3   &   ah   4   &   ah

Known as "The Master of Touch and Tone," **Jerry Byrd** is one of the most influential steel guitarists of all time. Although he does not play the steel guitar with pedals, he nonetheless has been a major influence on most everyone playing the pedal steel today. Byrd recorded with Hank Williams, Marty Robbins, Red Foley and many others in the 1950s before falling under the spell of Hawaiian music and devoting his time to playing and recording many albums in the Hawaiian style. He was inducted into the Steel Guitar Hall of Fame in 1978.

Swing Eighth Notes

Often, we want blues tunes to have a swaying, swinging feel. To accomplish this, we use *swing eighth* notes. To play swing eighth notes, connect the first two notes of a triplet with a tie.

This can also be written like so:

Generally, swing eighth notes are written like normal eighth notes and musicians swing them as appropriate. Sometimes there is an instruction at the beginning of the music to play swing 8ths. In this book, we'll use *Swing 8ths.*

The next song is made from the minor pentatonic scale. Practice it slowly and watch out for bars 9

and 10, which include the C pedal and can be tricky.

Blues Walkin'   Track 73

Swing 8ths

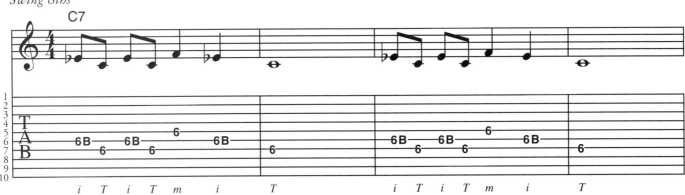

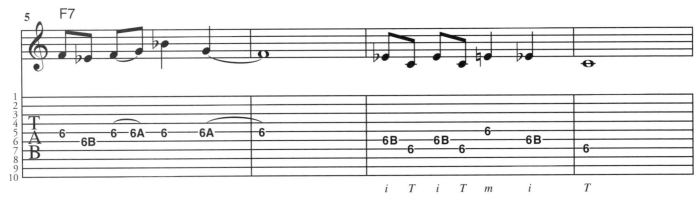

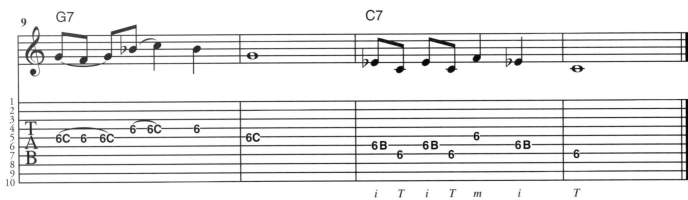

NASHVILLE NUMBER SYSTEM

Not confined to Nashville, the *number system* was developed by professional musicians as a way to make it easier to play songs in any key by substituting numbers for chord symbols. This is needed because not all singers will sing a song in the same key. Rather than memorizing songs in every key, the musician simply has to know what key to play in and follow the chord numbers.

Let's take a look at how the number system works.

It is important to have a good understanding of the chords in a major key and their qualities (major, minor, dominant), as the number system is based upon this knowledge.

The number system replaces chord symbols with corresponding numbers based upon the major scale.

Memorize the following information, and the system will work for you:

   1, 4 and 5 are major chords
   2, 3 and 6 are minor
   7 is diminished (Root–$\flat$3–$\flat$5)

Here is the number system applied to the key of C Major.

C Major scale:	C	D	E	F	G	A	B	C
Numbers:	1	2	3	4	5	6	7	1

Let's use a 12-bar blues progression as an example. On the left is the chord progression using chord symbols. On the right is the same progression using the numbering system.

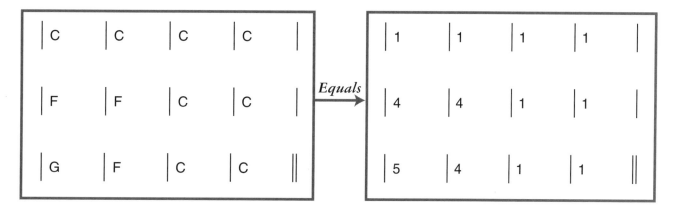

Next we will look at how the
number system labels minor and
dominant chords.

A dominant 7th chord built on G would be written G7. In the number system G is 5 in the key of C Major, so in that key, G7 would be written 5^7.

Minor chords are typically written like this: Dmin or D-. In the number system, the minor chord is identified by a small m. Since Dmin is 2 in the key of C Major, Dmin would be 2m.

The following example will show how the system works with the different types of chords. Here is a traditional lead sheet for a chord progression in C Major.

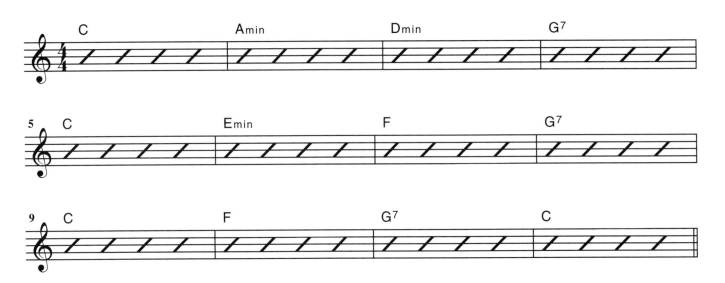

With the number system, this becomes:

1	6 m	2 m	5^7	
1	3 m	4	5^7	
1	4	5^7	1	‖

FINAL WORDS

Practicing

Approached with a plan and a goal, practicing can be both a fun and rewarding experience.

Decide where you want to go with the pedal steel guitar. Is your goal to play in a band or jam occasionally with some friends? If your answer is that you want to play in a band, then you will most likely be learning the hit songs heard on the radio. If your answer is to jam with your friends occasionally, then you get to learn all of your favorite songs, new or old. When you have a long-term goal, it can be achieved by setting lots of small, short-term, easily attainable goals. By setting a series of small goals, you won't become over-whelmed and lose heart. Nothing breeds success like success!

Practice Tools

Playing a musical instrument is supposed to be fun right? It is! And these days there are some great practice aids to keep it enjoyable.

The most essential practice tool is the *metronome*, which is an adjustable device that marks musical time. This will help you keep a steady beat. Metronomes can be as simple as a unit that plays a "click" all the way up to metronomes that subdivide the beats with different sounding clicks.

Another way to keep a steady beat is to play along with a *drum machine*. This is a fun and realistic way to practice. Drum machines come in all shapes and sizes, from hardware units to software that can be loaded onto your computer. Check with your local music store to see and try out some of the different types.

Background tracks, such as the Stand Alone Tracks products from the National Guitar Workshop and Alfred, are also a fun and very realistic way to go. These allow you to play along with a band playing in the style you choose. This is a great way to put the techniques you have been learning to use. There are many sources of background tracks, so check with your music store and do some research on the Internet. Most stores that specialize in the pedal steel guitar have background tracks that are specifically tailored for the pedal steel guitar player.

Okay, you have a metronome and drum machine and love the back-ground tracks. You have been practicing scales and the songs and licks in this book. Where do you go from there?

Just about every musician has learned songs, licks and techniques from recordings they admire at some point. This is a time-tested way of learning to play a musical instru-ment. Learning to play what has come before (even if it was only yesterday) is a major part of develop-ing your own style.

Learning a solo and maybe a few key licks from a song can be an eye-opening experience. The more you do it the easier it will get, the better you will sound and the more fun you will have!

Another good practice tool is a recording device. By occasionally recording yourself playing along with your metronome, drum machine or background track, you will learn where you need additional work and also what sounds good. Recordings don't lie, but try not to be discouraged if you don't like what you hear. Sometimes, walking away and coming back to listen with fresh ears is all that is needed. When listening back to your recording, take note of what needs improve-ment. Then, set about correcting weaknesses in a positive way.

Summary

Setting small, attainable goals and using a metronome or some other timekeeping device will get you on your way to becoming a proficient pedal steel guitar player. In addition to the recordings of your playing, keeping a journal of your practice sessions is a great way to see where you have been and what needs to be done to accomplish your goals.

So, practice slowly and methodically, set goals and above all, have fun!